[redacted]

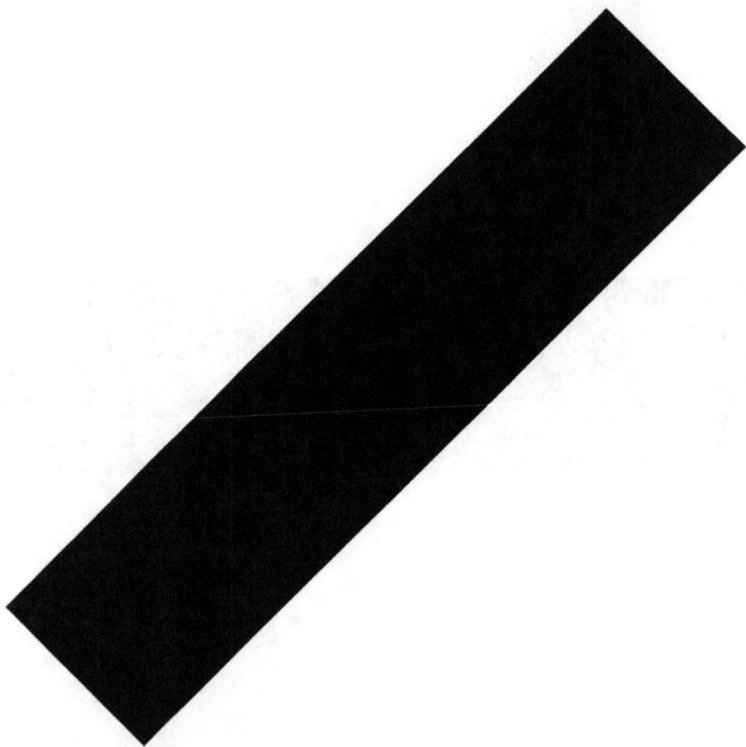

CLEANING CHURCH TOILETS

ryan miller

mangoink

Mango Ink Publishing

Mango Ink,

ISBN: 978-0989545426

Printed in the United States of America

Cover Art: Ryan Miller
Design and Layout: Ryan Miller

[redacted]

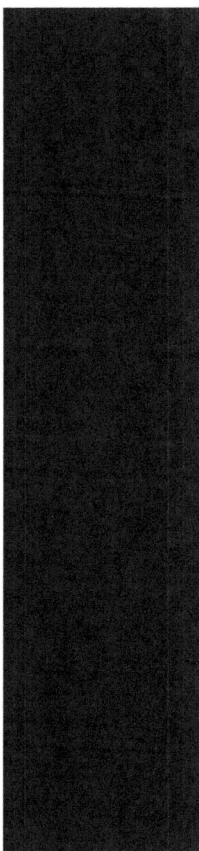

in

fish.

I think we humans are basically like these little cave fish I recently learned about that live in the cave Cueva del Azufre, in southern Mexico. The little guys have been subject to some fairly brutal treatment for hundreds of years. The Zoque, an indigenous people in the area, believe that the fish are a gift from the gods of the underworld. Gods of the underworld sounds pretty terrifying, honestly, but these gods of the underworld are also the gods that send rain to feed the crops the Zoque grow in southern Mexico. The crops that enable them to survive.

So every year (before being banned by the Mexican government) the Zoque performed a small ceremony with these fish at the end of dry season, the week before Easter (interesting timing).

Though it's not exactly what I expected someone to do with a gift from a god, the Zoque poison the water that the fish live in. They grind up the roots of the Barbasco plant to create a paste (with a touch of lime juice of course) and drop it into the dark pools of the cave. The fish end up interacting with the toxin - which paralyzes them - and the Zoque scoop them out of the poisoned water, kill them and eat them until their meals of fish can be replaced with the new line of crops that will eventually arrive- thanks to an abundance of rain from the gods of the underworld.

Apparently, the fish don't taste especially great - which makes sense since they were swimming in poison before being captured and eaten.

Much more interesting than anything up this point (which is all very interesting), is what these fish have done with being poisoned for years by people who believe in primitive gods and a religious system that has caused them to suffer every year right before Easter...

they have evolved.

They've changed. They've adapted. They're becoming immune to the toxins that paralyze them.

Some researchers took fish from that particular cave and fish from another area and exposed them to the same Barbasco plant poison. They found that the fish from the cave were much more able to withstand the poisons than those from other locations. They were able to keep swimming 50% longer. Some predict that if the ritual hadn't been banned, eventually the fish would have become immune to the poison.

I sometimes feel like one of those fish, and I don't think I'm the only one. It feels like I've been swimming in a world awash with religious, political, and economical systems and gods that have poisoned the environment. I don't think the answer is throwing away religion, politics or economy but I do think the answer is to evolve. I think we have to do some major adapting in our understanding of how to make this world work for us and how to resist the, often toxic, religious, political and economic, affects.

The philosopher Peter Rollins says something to the effect of "A letter always reaches its intended destination: the person who wrote it." The author and thinker Seth Godin writes something similar "The most important book you'll ever read, is the one you write."

(Tangent side note: this means you should probably start creating that thing you keep smothering in self-doubt and fear and anxiety. Your soul needs it. We need it too, but even if we didn't, the amount you need it should outweigh any benefit from the world needing it. Which, by the way, if everyone lived that way, the world would definitely benefit.)

Back to my main point: this book is about evolution and change and adaptation: my own evolution and change and adaptation. It began as a series of blog posts that changed quite a bit in the time I worked on them and the time I actually posted them - which just enforces all the more, that change can go pretty fast sometimes. Sometimes we need to stop and appreciate the evolution. Think about the adaptation. Smell the change. Feel the growth. Say hello and get to know the new thing we've become so that we can continue to survive and get stronger. And continue to change.

And probably ask some questions to confirm that all this change is for the better.

At the time of this writing, almost 8 years ago, as chance would have it, I became a pastor. I had worked in video games and, to make a long story short, going from video games to preaching sermons was a fairly big change.

People change jobs all the time. But when you have to suddenly start talking to people about religion, spirituality, toxins, and gods... you find yourself thinking a lot about religion, spirituality and gods more than you did when making video games. Or at least in a certain... church(y) way, which I also wasn't sure I liked. I generally don't like church(y) things.

I grew up in the church so the landscape was not too foreign. My dad was a pastor. My dad was a dad, first, then a pastor. My dad didn't make me go to youth group even though it looked bad on him. But my dad was also a pastor and he had to sell his $1700 Porsche and buy a $2800 Geo Metro because the people at the church weren't sure him driving a Porsche "looked good".

As a teenager that makes you think religion is fairly stupid, especially because that Porsche was really fun to drive and that Geo Metro... was not.

People have much worse stories than that about church. I've heard about the trauma and tragedy and abuse repeatedly. I could write a very depressing book about it.

But we all know the water is filled with poison. That conversation, to be honest, is boring at best and carries its own toxicity at worst.

My parents, I've realized fairly recently, instilled in me a freedom to pursue change. They would never say it this way, but they taught me, and modeled, the pursuit of evolution, even spiritual evolution. I'm grateful to them for that.

All kinds of words get thrown around when religious people begin to evolve or change… to find the narrow paths that branch off the wide path. Sometimes those words are heretic and false prophet. Sometimes they even kill the heretical, false prophet who talks about the life found on the narrow path and the destruction found on the wide.

I wish we could find a way to use evolutionary instead of heretical and false. Revolutionary would work too. (Those words generally do work in the portions of life where change is expected and celebrated - like science.) If we go back to the story of those cave fish, the only other viable option to change is death.

I think many forms of Christianity are dying. I don't think I'm the only one who thinks this. But I also think that if cave fish who can't deal with toxic religion are the forms of Christianity who are dying, well I wish they would die sooner. Of course, the form of Christianity that we currently think is the "correct" form once evolved from a worse form, dating back... well to the advent of humanity. Religious followers have thought many times throughout their history that they finally had it figured out... only to see some other generation come and figure it out again for the last time.

Evolution is a requirement for any kind of legitimate faith.

People always start to ask the questions they aren't supposed to ask, read the books they aren't supposed to read, trust the people they aren't supposed to trust, have thoughts they aren't supposed to think, listen to people they aren't supposed to listen to, find truth where they aren't supposed to search, knock on doors they aren't supposed to open... you get the picture. They keep asking, seeking, and knocking... and that's always dangerous to some.

That's what I did. That's what I continue to do.

I bet those cave fish that started to adapt to toxins were told by all their fish friends to stop changing and to continue to be like everyone else... just before those old friends, who refused to change, passed out and were scooped up to be eaten.

So these chapters (originally a series of blog posts) called "Cleaning Church Toilets" are a reflection on my changes, in a sense. I know I have all kinds of biases, blind spots, and prejudices and I'm trying to be more aware of them. I've learned that when we give space to thoughts and life and change, they grow and we grow in all the right ways.

And so this is for me. Am I happy where I'm at? Where am I at? What do I think of all this? How have things changed? What have I learned? Am I evolving? What am I communicating? Who am I now?

These will be mostly concise ideas and experiences that have stood out to me over the past 9 years or so, that have infected me, transformed me, and, moved me as I've talked, listened, lead, and cleaned toilets.

In fact, a few Sundays ago someone came up to me and said, "Ryan, the men's bathroom..."

I responded, with a smile, "Yeah, it's right over there."

"No," they smiled back. "The toilet is plugged and there's water everywhere."

"Oh. Right."

It's always good that people can trust you with some of their deepest secrets… and to unplug their toilets.

So, I unplugged the toilet, again. And I mopped the floor, again. And I thought why do I do this? Again. And I remembered, why. Again.

My hope, of course, is that my change syncs up with your change in one way or another. My hope is that it inspires you, challenges you, gets you mad, gets you glad, encourages, empowers and all of the other things that my evolution has done to me as I've looked back.

We can't just keep swimming in this pond and letting the poisons get to us, right?

If it's not obvious, let me say it outright: I don't have it all figured out.

I didn't a year ago. I still don't. I won't a year from now.

Change doesn't rest. Evolution doesn't become satisfied. New never gives way to mediocre. The wine-skins always get old at some point but fortunately this universe always has something new around its ever expanding corner. Even religiously speaking.

So, even as I take a second to ponder where I've come from and what it means for me now, I get excited about what is to come. I hope you do too.

001

words.

I have three brothers. I am the youngest of four boys. My brothers and I are all very different and sometimes I wonder how we all grew up under the same parents.

I have a brother who wears graphic tees, flannels, and hats and is one of the most talented artists I'm aware of. He's one of the most creative people I've ever met. He's also, last I checked, an Atheist. I recently had a discussion with him as to whether we, as humans, are anything more than brains. What about energy? What about those mysterious hidden realms? No, he thinks we are all brain. I love this brother an incredible amount.

I have a brother who wears tweed jackets, and smokes a pipe. He as two Master's Degrees and one PhD (more schooling than the rest of the brothers combined) and he enjoys all things British. I would say, last I checked, he's on the conservative side of Christianity. I've had many conversations with him about art... and I usually run for the hills because I can't keep up. He's pretty black and white. I love this brother an incredible amount.

I have a brother who is somewhere in the middle of these other brothers (if middle is between conservative Christianity and atheism) and he's probably the closest to where I stand. (As chance would have it, we were also born on the same day.) He loves science, reason and logic but also goes with "feeling" as pretty important. I love this brother an incredible amount.

So, I have 3 very different brothers.

This means at least a couple of things:

1. I'm rarely shocked that someone disagrees with me. Heck, I'm shocked if they don't. I don't know that there is one thing on this planet that the four of us brothers would all agree on in regards to politics, theology, art, sociology, culture, psychology, places to live, places to go, and definitely what a good movie is. We always disagree and we let each other know.

2. They have made me. I respect Atheism and I respect a conservative form Christianity. I don't agree with them but I recognize I've come from them. I learn from them. I appreciate them.

I once fasted (from eating) so George W. Bush would be elected. I've fasted twice in my life and one of them was for the election of a politician. Unreal. If you know me now, you find that astounding.

At one time, I had a concealed weapons permit and carried a .45 caliber gun around town in a holster and in my car. I packed heat. If you know me now, you find that one of the most unbelievable statements on the planet.

I once cheered that the "gay kid" was thrown through a window by someone in High School. I've said things about homosexuality that I won't even tell you I said, just because saying it isn't worth it and I'm more than embarrassed of what I used to say and how I used to treat certain people.

I once felt nervous about Catholics, let alone Muslims and Buddhists, who were going to Hell and could pull me along if I wasn't careful.

At best, I was a Republican, 2nd Amendment supporter, Protestant, proud heterosexual. At worst, I was a judgmental, arrogant, proud, bigot who knew the answer to everything in the world... or at least who to ask if I didn't have the answer. And who not to ask for any answers.

And then I became the one I was not supposed to ask.

I have a cousin who brags to her friends that I'm one of the few people who has completely changed as an adult. It's one of the coolest things anyone has ever said about me. (I don't think I'm the only one by any stretch but it's cool to be in that rare group.)

I don't say all of this to say that I'm enlightened, or that I've arrived, or that if you are a supporter of the things I once was (besides being mean to any group of people) that I'm better than you. I don't say this to say that my brothers are right or wrong or better or worse.

I do say it all to say... what changed me? What changes any of us? What makes them who they are and me who I am?

There are all kinds of factors, obviously, but at the end of the day, at some level, at a most basic level, it's amazing to think the powerful part that some combination of words plays in all of this.

Just words. Words spoken, words written, words thrown back and forth in conversation. But, still, just words.

There is that little saying that sticks and stones can break bones but words can't hurt anyone. It's a pretty ironic statement: using words to help someone who has been hurt by words to feel better. The statement enforces the power of words even while trying to say they are meaningless.

We all know they aren't meaningless. Words are, in fact, one of the building blocks of who we are and what we are. They are as essential to the universe as electrons and protons.

The first time that we officially started thinking about a new church, as a group of people, there were 10 of us in a living room and we all wrote down words on 3 x 5 cards. We wrote down words that we hoped would describe the new church-thing we were hoping to start.

After merging together similar ideas, we ended up with 4 words: safe, simple, risky, and giving. (We added together later.) It's not that the words themselves are that amazing, it's that organizations start with words at all and those words formed a group of people and their culture for years to come.

Just words.

There is a fairly well-known story about Johnny Cash. His older brother died at the age of twelve in a terrible accident and Johnny's father apparently blamed Johnny (who was ten at the time). A father told a ten year-old that it should have been the ten year-old who had died instead of his brother. Many, including Johnny's kids, say it was those words that never left Johnny and made him the artist he was.

Just words. Haunted a man until his death. And formed him.

I have a friend whose father told her repeatedly that the world would have been better off she had not been born and another friend whose mother told her, repeatedly, it was a mistake she had been born.

Just words.

There are stories that determine how I try to live, and I am not alone. More words. Myths, stories, fables have formed so much of our histories and progress it's sometimes amazing to think what would exist if it were not for them. Anything?

I only say all of this because I have met many people who have had prisons built around them because of words. I've also met people who have been freed from prisons because of words.

Words - just words - are still affecting us. They are opening people up, making the world bigger, helping us all to be more aware, more optimistic, more inspired, and more creative.

Words - just words - are limiting people, making them feel small, creating wounds, and damaging societies and cultures and killing us all.

Just words. Harmless little words with no power compared to sticks and stones.

Humanity, often times in a religious nature, has used words in many of the wrong ways throughout its history. The words created a destructive and toxic environment to swim in. The effect of those words still lives everywhere in churches. And they are perhaps deadlier, longer, in those worlds than in other worlds.

Those words bother me more than any others. Their effect haunts me because I've seen what they do to people, first hand. I've seen the prisons, the spiritual insane asylums, and the devastation they reap. They are the Nazgul, the Dementors, the monsters of the night, terrorizing human beings everywhere. The Dark Words.

This is a book, obviously, made of words. I love words. I love speaking them and listening to them. I love how they are born and how they live inside each of us and our unique perspectives of this world.

I hope that wherever words have been used to trap you, haunt you, and cause you to be afraid, you can find some freedom, some inspiration and something new with other words, including the words that will appear here.

002

meanings.

Not too long ago I received an email that was pretty critical of me. This, of course, has happened before, but it's also not an every day event. Either way, it always stings - words hurt.

This particular letter used words like agnosticism, atheism, humanism, belief and teachings, disprove, Christian, archaic text and imaginary savior.

The gist was that I can't be who I really am at church, or say what I really want to say - which is a humanist, agnostic, potential atheist - because my livelihood is tied up into trying to bring some credibility to my Christian biases.

To sum up: someone considers me to be fake.

No one likes to be called fake. But I really don't. Especially as a pastor. Pastors have been known as fake for as long as water has been known as wet. I despise the connotation. But I tried to listen anyway. I read the email many times.

To be honest, after thinking about it, the only way I could respond to the email was "What do you mean by all those words? You might be exactly right but I'm not sure." I don't think I'm fake, but depending on the author's definition of the words used, I could potentially understand how he/she might think so.

After some back and forth emails the person writing told me I had "big balls". So, I went from "fake" 'to "big balled" which, again,

I'm not exactly sure what it all means.

Or how about this one? A requirement for a foundation of Christian faith is "Faith in the divinity of the historic Christ (not only prophet and perfect man, but also object of love and worship)."

Agree? Disagree? Depending on what we mean by divinity, faith, historic, and Christ I might agree. You might.

But, I also might not. You might not.

And this is so much of my life. Well... what does that word mean? I might agree. Or might not, depending on... This is so many of the conversations with my brothers... well what do you mean by beauty, by truth, by art, by good?

I've fallen in love with the word polysemous. (Not a sentence I thought I would ever type.) My friend Matthew Roy (master of Russian Literature, piano, and many other things) introduced it to me in some emails we were sending back and forth.

Polysemous refers to words with many meanings - like bank, crane, speaker, or bat (if it's not immediately obvious read those words again).

But there are many more words with multiple meanings than just the obvious. Here are a few I have found to be pretty important:

God.
Sin.
Hell.
Holy.
Salvation.
Justice.
Heretic.
Christian.
Pastor.
Righteous.

Church.
Stupid.
Weird.
Art.
Safe.
Success.
School.
Ready.
American.
Responsibility.
Love.

We could go through the entire list but what if we just start with the word "god"? Every human being either believes in a god, doesn't believe in a god, or isn't sure if they believe in a god and the word "god" might be the most polysemous word ever spoken.

What the hell does god mean?

Zeus, Allah, or Mystery?

How do we know what we do, don't, or might believe in? We could probably tell an Atheist they do believe in a god and a Theist that they don't, depending on how we define god. (Ignosticism might be on to something here with the claim that both Theists and Atheists are off until they define the concept of the word they are both using.)

Even if I think I'm using the right word, someone else may think something completely different than what I had hoped. When I use a word today, it might mean something different than when I used the same word a few years ago and I will probably mean something different in a few years from now. And that's just for me and my perception of words via my culture, experience, and perspective.

Which makes language and our use of words (and their power)

even more fragile, and yet, powerful than we think.

There is an aversion to some words, no matter how right a definition, because of past pain and trauma associated with them. Others may say the same word has "saved" their life. They are in love with the word and will express bewilderment at anyone who "doesn't know what they mean" or finds the definition offensive.

All of the words on the list above are prime examples of both of these experiences. There are words that we just don't want to have a relationship with anymore and we can't understand why anyone would. And there are words that we are so in love with that we can't understand why anyone wouldn't love them as much as we do.

Put all of this together and you end up with some interesting combinations of words. How about this fine collection: "My pastor at church tells me that god loves me and has granted me salvation from hell if I repent of my sin and that I will be righteous and holy and go to heaven where there will be no heretics because god is full of justice. Jesus died for my sins. God Bless America..."

I honestly have absolutely no idea what that means because it could, quite literally, mean anything… but I can also honestly tell you I have a strong distaste for everything about that paragraph. The words are stained and toxic. Still, if you gave me 10 minutes, I could agree with them with certain definitions of the words... definitions that not everyone might agree with.

So, words matter, and yet, they can't matter. Not to the extent that religion has made them matter.

They are... just words.

And often excuses. We sometimes throw them out like a flare hoping they will distract from the missile headed toward our deeper selves or our perceived responsibilities - a distraction from the things we don't understand or don't really want to talk about. A perceived solution to our shame... that only make us feel more unworthy in the end because we're faking what we're even saying.

Of course, I believe in Jesus! Now stop asking me any more questions about things that actually matter... like... what does it mean to believe in Jesus.

We can speak so many words but what do we really know?

And yet, I'm asking all of these questions... with words.

I don't know.

It feels like the world gets a little lighter every time they are uttered by a human being.

I don't know.

Wait, what? You don't know either? Thank God.

003

Christianity is a word.

Speaking of I don't know...

Christianity? What does that mean?

I know I'm a Christian the way many Christians define it but I also know I'm not a Christian the way many Christians define it, which means that instead of knowing whether I'm a Christian, or not, I only know that no one really agrees on what a Christian even is.

I've had many conversations with people who are worried they are no longer a "Christian" and by the time we're done, I think it's fantastic news.

I've had other conversations with people who tell me that they would never become a "Christian" and by the time we're done, I think they are already more "Christian" than the majority of "Christians" that I know.

Am I a Christian? Is this a Christian writing? I don't know.

There are many who say you can't be a Catholic and be a Christian which is kinda like saying you can't be a Tiger and be a Cat... but you won't change their mind. (And there are probably some who would insist that a Tiger is not a Cat.)

I've spent some time thinking about why this even matters to me. Who cares? Use the word or don't. I'm not sure any of this would really matter if it weren't for my own ego. Which might say something about the value I still place on the word and its ties to my ego.

We can all relate. It's frustrating when someone comes along claiming to be in our "tribe" whom we don't think is in our tribe, or we don't want in our tribe. They make us and our tribe look bad and so we get angry and defensive and afraid and then we worry about definitions.

We don't need to look any further than "You're not a real American." Technicalities and definitions don't matter. Perceptions do.

To a small degree it's how my Muslim friend feels when he hears someone talk about ISIS as an Islamic group. He gets angry. He gets upset. He tries to explain definitions and uses words like "true" and "real" which only illustrate how desperate we all our to define these things of which we see ourselves as a part.

All of it, including myself and my anger is just religious tribal ego and it's amazing how violent the religious tribal ego can get about defending definitions.

Because, again, what does it mean to be a Christian?

Words like follow, believe, Jesus, have all the same problems. Even the Bible speaks of "believing in Jesus" and yet "demons believing" and "faith without works" and "saved by grace".

And Jesus talks about wind and birth and tells stories to try and explain this "kingdom of God"… all of which is very vague and hard to pin down.

All that to say that some will assume, people will criticize, people will reject, people will pay attention... and there isn't any label I can use that won't have a similar spectrum of responses.

So, I do use Christian to describe myself and our church. It's my culture, and the language I'm most comfortable with (even if some of it is toxic)

But I also think that many people who use the word Christian should be using the word Pharisee.

And I do have my own definition of the word Christian.

004

the news.

My great friend Kent and I were having a beer in Michigan. Kent has a Doctorate of Ministry from Carey Theological Seminary and a Masters of Divinity from Gordon Conwell Seminary. Plenty of education.

I was a pastor at the time. I was preaching on Sundays. I had been a "Christian" all my life although, admittedly, I have very little education (if education means Degrees).

Our conversation was around "What is the good news (or gospel)?" or "What is Christianity?" We were trying to come up with a definition... which is pretty telling, since we would both call ourselves that word.

It was astounding how hard it was for both of us to answer that question without going down all kinds of rabbit trails and complications.

Good news seems pretty easy to define. It's something you haven't heard and it's good. You just won the lottery! You just won a free trip to Australia! You won first place! (It's telling how often our examples of good have to do with winning something...)

Years later, I was in a college level class (taught by Kent) where students were trying to answer similar questions and they were watching YouTube videos, listening to lectures and trying to get it down to three minutes.

This was in a class where everyone had the same definition, for the most part, of the words in the definition, and they were struggling to agree on the good news and get it down to three minutes.

Three minutes?

"You're cancer free" takes 1 second and is pretty good (even fantastic) news.

If Christianity is centered around the "good news" and the good news is as complicated as it seems, well... I mean... I know why I'm not sure I'm a Christian and I know why so many people feel like me. Or worse, disinterested.

Do you want to be a Christian?

Yes!

What does that mean?

I'm not sure. Agree to some words?

Which has all made me think through this whole thing quite a bit, especially since I'm seen as some kind of spokesmen for this thing. And I've come up with my definition.

Ready?

You're enough.

Yeah, that's it. That's my definition. I understand that's it not really a definition but more of a statement but I think Christianity is more of a statement than a definition anyway.

I do have a slightly longer version for those that need it:

You are valuable, you are worthy, you are beautiful, you are powerful. You are love. There is nothing more that needs to be done or can be done to make the authentic you any more of those things.

Believe it. Accept it. Have faith in it.

Some might ask where Jesus is in that definition and that's a very fair question since Jesus is pretty much the main character of Christianity.

My response would be that Jesus is everywhere in it.

005

the truth is in you. the darkness is fading. the light is already shining.

Many, when they hear or read things like "Christianity can be summed up with the two words, "you're enough" will say "that's not what the Bible says". I get that. To a degree.

But saying "that's not what the Bible says" implies a certain understanding of the Bible. A more Google-like understanding.

If you've ever been in an conversation about who won the 2012 Best Actor award, someone will eventually says "Google it". Then the disagreement ends. Many view the Bible the same way.

What is the definition of a Christian? Bible it. Disagreement over.

Unfortunately, the Bible rarely works this way, even when asking facts... "How many stalls of horses did Solomon have?" (The Bible actually gives two answers for that one. Whoops.)

And this is not just a Christian problem. Everyone uses this thing as though it's some database of answers. (We'll get into all of that later but, for now, it's not!)

That's not to say it doesn't have some amazing words in it. Like the name of this chapter.

The first time I came across these words, I couldn't stop reading them. They just jumped off the page. The optimism, the inspiration, the shouts of "enough". I *think* they are true but I also *want* them to be true. They are empowering just to read.

A guy named John wrote the words and they found their way into the Bible. The same Bible that says some pretty terrible things has phrases like the one above.

Read them again, just for fun.

I've spent a lot of my life trying to cause certain things to happen. I've learned it's more worthwhile spending my time trying to become more aware of what is already happening and I think the Bible has been trying to tell that story for a long time.

You are valuable,
you are worthy,
you are beautiful,
you are powerful.

You are love.
There is nothing more that needs to be done
or can be done
to make the authentic you
any more of those things.

006

the lie.

The creation myth is the first "story" in the Bible.

I use myth purposefully: that story has so much truth that is way beyond whether or not it actually happened. No one ever asks if Little Red Riding Hood really did meet a talking wolf because no one needs to. We all know that's not the point of the truth.

The Bible's "creation" myth is a poetic birthing story meant to inform us of greater truths of the deepest parts of humanity, and our own birthing. It's not meant to throw out superficial scientific facts... and arguing for that appears as empty as arguing that the boy really did cry wolf even though we don't have scientific evidence.

That birthing poem/myth is one of my favorites because it is so layered. Like any good story, there are so many ways to come at it: Rest. Work. Creativity. Shame. Fear.

The story, the myth, the tale, the poem, begins with all kinds of good. In fact, everything is good or very good as the story tells us. "Good" is sprinkled everywhere. Good is also a word that could mean a lot of things but it generally doesn't mean perfect. Some people would even say that their pain has been good. (But more on that later.)

I think every human story begins with good. I have lots of theologians and scholars to back me up on this too. It's known as Original Blessing. The stories start off good. But, because it's always easier to sell a solution for something messed up than to sell that you're good enough without me or my answers, the concept of Original Sin won the popularity battle.

But even though the story is "all good" I can't deny that there is something not good in that story of humanity, and in our stories. (Depending on our definition of "good", "not good" could mean all kinds of things too.)

Still, things go from good to not good. There is a trajectory that I don't think most humans want. No matter definitions, when things go from good to not good in a story, I pay attention. Things go from good to not good in just about every story, and we call these things, conflict, tension, antagonists, and struggle. As much as we hate things going from good to not good, it's what makes a story relevant and powerful, because it happens all the time.

And we also learn the most in that part of the story. That's where the meat is.

What brings about the "not good" in the birthing story of the Bible is a thought of the main characters: a perspective. A way of viewing themselves and the world. They didn't think they were enough. They believed that there was more to be done to become "enough".

Of course, there is a "voice" telling them they are not enough. There always is and you can call the voice anything you like: the accuser, the ego, the "devil", a snake, or just "evil"... it's the voice that tells us that we aren't enough. The voice keeps yelling that there is something missing and something better to get to in terms of our standings with the gods.

If either of those are true then we are not enough just where we are.

Once we believe that lie, we generally make another error, at least according to the story. We think that a great way to get to “enough” is to have knowledge... of good and evil. To get more of something than we have, to become like something else.

I don’t think the story is saying we shouldn’t learn. Although I do think there is a tremendous danger in learning so much that you become trapped in certainty. Still, not the point.

If you ask me, one of the primary reasons we want knowledge of good and evil, especially when we need to make ourselves feel more worthy, is to use that new-found knowledge on someone else. We usually want to put head knowledge about good and evil in our brains so that we can use that information as a bullet to take down people around us. If they go down, we are up and when we are more up, we make ourselves feel worthy again... at least compared to them... to make up for that first mistake in thinking. Even if they aren’t down, at least we have learned something to get us up.

This leads to a never ending cycle of work, pain, thorns, desire, jealousy and, of course, using our new-found knowledge to point out how bad others are, or at least how good we are.

It’s his fault. He’s bad. It’s her fault. She’s bad. It’s that snake’s fault. That snake is bad.

And since he’s bad, that means I’m better than him, right?

Am I more than enough now? Or at least back to enough?

It’s a dangerous path the story talks about. It can be a kind of hell when all humans do is look for brain knowledge to take down others to make themselves feel better. Or even when they look for certainty to make themselves feel better about uncertainty.

Unfortunately, religion did more to exacerbate the problem than to diminish it and by the time Jesus got here he was telling some religious leaders (Pharisees) that they were traveling over land and sea to create Sons of Hell. (Or participants in a world where all you do is look for knowledge to take down others to make yourself feel better to be enough... a.k.a. judgmental)

But, of course, we still love stories because after they go from good to not good, we know there is better good coming if we can just get through that fall or pit or desert, learning what we are supposed to.

I think Jesus came to stop all this madness and remind us that we're okay, we're enough, we're powerful, we're beautiful, we are love, and there is nothing we can do to be any more of those things. When we die to more, we find life. If we don't think we are enough already, well... we've lived this story before, right?

I think the point is to change the story when we live it. To not believe the lie.

007

a point.

For the first time in my life I have a spiritual director. I'm not always sure of the difference between a spiritual director/therapist/mentor/counselor/life coach, but either way I have a spiritual director: a Jesuit Priest whom I adore.

The other day, while listening to his questions, I had an epiphany of sorts: I've never planned much of anything. It's not my style.

I generally don't get real into vision statements, life statements, purpose statements, or goal-oriented-future-casts. I'm more run with the wind (sometimes literally) and go through doors that magically open for me. Or run by the doors that don't open.

I don't think this makes me an especially great business person and I do think it leaves people who ask me things like, "Where do you want to be in five years?" really disappointed. I also think it drives me to spiritual direction to try and figure out if I should change that part of my personality or, at least, get better at discerning long-term future ideas. Or maybe not. But it's worth asking.

I have recently come up with some words, for now, that I hope broaden my present and drive me into my future:

Help people (myself included) know the reality of who we are and what we are capable of.

That's Enough.

800

to know or not to know.

The way I grew up, and generally most people who grew up with a Western mindset, is to believe that knowing amounts to acknowledging something in my brain.

Knowing god, meant knowing things about god, although it was rarely explicitly said that way.

In the East, from what I have learned, knowing amounts to experiencing something.

So knowing god, means experiencing god.

Who knew that the definition of what it means to "know" can change everything?

Jean-Pierre de Caussade goes so far to say that some forms of knowledge, not only don't mean very much but they make real knowledge even worse.

When one is thirsty one quenches one's thirst by drinking, not by reading books which treat of this condition. The desire to know does but increase this thirst.

I think we generally know this. If you want to know how to ski, you don't read books about skiing. If you want to know how to write, you don't read books about writing.

If you want to know God, you don't read books about God?

When one is thirsty one quenches one's thirst by drinking, not by reading books which treat of this condition. The desire to know does but increase this thirst.

If one wants to know god, reading books about god, like the Bible, might be the worst way to do that... and only leave the reader more thirsty for something "real" (an experience).

Or going to seminary to gain a bunch of head knowledge, has the possibility of really pushing someone back from actually gaining the kind of knowledge that matters. (My dad, who went to seminary, calls this cementary, and the cement is not a good thing.)

If we bring the varying concepts of god into the definition of "know", we get a whole bunch of really interesting things to think about what people might be referring to when they say that someone needs to "know god".

It could mean that someone should acknowledge a bunch of information in their brain that doesn't really amount to much and actually might be preventing them from real knowledge or it could mean they should experience "the metaphor of the mystery that transcends all categories of human thought including being and non-being" to paraphrase Joseph Campbell.

And, of course, a whole host of other things.

God, as I define God, seemed pretty intent on constantly trying to remind humans that a knowledge of God is not nearly as powerful as an awareness of God because awareness of something is that different kind of knowledge that leads to experience.

600

it's important to know but not like that.

Most arguments or disagreements center around beliefs. I know this well.

My brothers and I, like I said, all agree on nothing.

I don't believe that was a good movie.
I don't believe he's a good director.
I don't believe he would make a good president or is a good president.
I don't believe God is like that, or exists, or loves those people.

We, as humans (myself included) often worry about losing our beliefs. What does that mean?

Some people feel the need to defend their beliefs, some people feel the need to attack and criticize beliefs. What does that mean?

I suppose the great thing about beliefs is that they are certain. We can easily quantify them and measure them. Do you believe like me? Yes or no. Are you in my tribe or not? Do I trust you? Are you like me? Should I be around you? Are you smarter, dumber, more liberal, more conservative?

What do you believe?

The dangerous thing is that, sometimes, certainty can be a cage. Beliefs can be a trap.

There is a saying, “Those who know, do not say; those who say, do not know.”

Carl Jung said his definition of reality is “that which affects you”.

Apparently, if people believe that a wine is an expensive wine, their brain will tell them that the wine tastes better. Their belief affects experience. Researchers have seen it in MRI machines. (After talking with some Alaskan fisherman, I’m convinced Copper River Salmon is the same phenomenon - it’s all in my brain.)

So beliefs matter.

Paul Coutinho says that if someone proved Jesus never existed, he would still die for the myth because in the East, “experience that affects life is truth”.

This is all pretty radical in the way that it forces us to confront what we believe, why we believe, and, maybe more importantly, what and why we experience.

I enjoyed this wine can be a more intriguing conversation than this wine is better.

I’ve found that conversations about beliefs are always much less interesting than conversations about experience. They are also much more uncertain, and thus, less argumentative and, thus, more instructive and helpful and unifying.

A story, it seems, is always more moving than an explanation.

A myth, it seems, is always more inspiring than a formula.

Human experience, it seems, is more meaningful than religious beliefs.

Making an effort to move conversations that center around beliefs to, at least, the beliefs that affect experience, if not the experiences themselves, seems to move conversations to more beneficial places.

Sadly, we hear more explanations, formulas, and religious beliefs in terms of God, than we do stories, myths, and experience. I think that's a problem.

010

knowing god is not.

Augustine: “If you comprehend it, it is not God.”

Aquinas: “Since we cannot know what God is, but only what God is not, we cannot consider how God is but only how He is not.”

Rabbi Kushner: Literally [God] means nothing. But with a capital N.

Richard Rohr: “We can only come to know God as we let go of our ideas about God, and as what is not God is stripped away.”

If we come back to that birthing creation story, those humans sought more knowledge because their awareness of what already was, was not enough.

They had enough experience. They were walking with God. But they didn’t think they had enough knowledge, and so they reached for more, and when we reach for more, it takes what we have.

Isn’t the point then, when we talk about “returning to the garden” to get back to what is true? To strip away? To remove? To realize?

As they say, the more you think you know, the less you know, and the less you think you know, the more you know.

Because knowing blocks knowing. Not knowing anything, is the most amazing way to know everything.

Not knowing is where evolution happens. Being uncertain is where truth is found. Admitting stupidity is where learning happens. Humility is the only place we can open ourselves up enough to receive. Realizing some of our fish friends are dying in the poisoned water is the only way we can adapt.

And we are most free to not know because we realize we are enough. Suddenly, everything is alright. Knowing is free to become what it is supposed to be... not a way to get there, but a way to realize.

I honestly think that everyone should be an agnostic of some kind or another. And I mean that. The only thing I know is that I don't need to know anything in order to be loved by this God of love.

And then I can start to change in freedom.

011

god?

I'll never forget Penny. Not only does the name remind me of LOST but Penny and I had one of those moments. I met her outside of a hospital, sitting on a little bench in the sun. She did most of the talking for the 45 minutes I knew her and she smoked three or four cigarettes,while telling me about her husband Mel who was in the hospital.

He had served in Vietnam and was living with the effects of Agent Orange. He was on dialysis and they'd just found cancer. Penny and Mel have been married for over 50 years. Penny told me about Mel's inability to sleep, she told me about having kids while Mel was stationed away, she told me about stories that still haunt Mel, she told me about her own mom dying when she was just a teenager and she told me about meeting Mel at a Roller Skating Rink.

I wish everyone could meet Penny. I wish I could accurately describe with words what it was like to hear her story.

My wife and kids recently returned from our own local skating rink (where I'm sure future Penny and Mels are meeting every day). At our own rink, there is a fairly legendary skater in his 70's who paints the floor with his wheels on a regular basis. The man is smooth like silk, he twists and twirls like no other on those brushes of motion. He's a joy to look at. You can't help but smile, those kind of smiles that only come out on rare moments.

I found myself outside of a thrift store with a man from Iraq, a man from Sudan, a woman from Russia and a man from Uzbekistan. The Iraqi and Sudanese had just met and were speaking Arabic to one another about finding a mechanic for a car. This was huge because the Iraqi was my friend and we were just trying to figure out what to do with his car that wasn't working. And a man from Sudan was the answer? A man brought there by a woman from Russia and a man from Uzbekistan. I almost broke down in tears of joy.

There was this old man on a beach in Mexico. White hair and tanned skin and a little bulge of a belly. He enjoyed food. Probably a beer from time to time. I'm a person who stares anyway, but this gentleman, I couldn't take my eyes off of him. It was as though there was no one else on the beach - even though it was packed. He walked very slowly, stood directly in front of me, and took off his pants in order to enter the ocean. He had on some shorts underneath. Everything he did was slow. Appreciative. Warm. He swam for a while, put back on his pants and walked away. Again, smiles like the one I wore as he left, don't come very often. I told everyone around to look at that man. I wondered if he was God.

God?

Of course not. Of course not. God isn't that. God is...

Well, what is God?

We should at least look to the Bible.

King
Judge
Shepherd
Rock
Lion
Fortress
Friend
Father

Co-worker
Potter
Wind
Breath
Vine
Light
Farmer
Old woman
Mother hen
Bride-groom
Fountain
Gate
Water
Bread
Fire

Is God a rock any more than God is a smoker outside a hospital?

Is God a vine any more than an elderly gentleman on skates?

Is God water any more than a conversation between refugees?

Is God a piece of bread any more than an old man on a beach?

012

where?

It's one of the most common questions I hear asked: where is God?

Where are you God? What are you doing? Do you notice the crap pile down here? Want to step in?

We can go on and on.

I was recently in a conversation with a pretty depressed person who asked another version of the question to me: Why God doesn't show up more often?

I don't know?

I know there are all kinds of answers but, if I'm honest, I've found most of them to feel pretty empty. But, in that conversation, I realized a more important question that isn't asked as often.

What does it look like when God does show up?

Is it powerful? What kind of power? Is it understood? Is it painting swatches of color across the sky? Is it fixing all the pain of the world?

Or is it mysterious. Is it weak? Is it vulnerability and love and does it live in all the places we don't think it should?

Is it evolving humans who live with suffering in order to evolve more?

I don't know.

But I do think the reason many of us don't see God is because many of us are too certain what, exactly, God looks like. Ironically enough, the main book about God, tried to make sure we never were too certain for just that reason.

Whenever people became too certain, god turned into an idol and they stopped seeing God because they were too focused on the representation of God.

I think God is always revealing God's self. I don't think that's the main problem. I think the bigger problem might be what we're expecting it to look like. As we all know, expectations make up a lot of our ability to see and experience.

013

human matters.

This is a big one for me. A huge perspective shift. I've thought a lot about it.

The way that I grew up, and the question that was usually the most important question to be able to answer, was the question around the divinity of Jesus. Was Jesus God? Is Jesus God? Fully God... A lot of things seemed to hinge on the answer to that question.

I don't think that's the important question anymore.

I think the important question is... Was Jesus fully human?

Now I realize that many Christians have, for years, said that Jesus was both fully God and fully human. The problem with that for me, was that it was impossible given what I was taught that God and humans were. I was taught God knows everything and humans don't. I was taught God was good and humans were evil. I was taught that God couldn't be around sin and humans were "original sin".

So, for any creature to be both God and human didn't really make sense. In fact, it was like saying a creature is a cat and a dog. And I'm all for things not making sense... but there is a line.

Really to say that Jesus was God didn't make much sense, because again, Jesus, for starters, said he didn't know things that the "Father" did.

And, of course, this all is determined by our definitions. Richard Rohr says that saying Jesus is God is heretical... because Jesus is a part of the trinity.

Okay... at some point I learned a different way of looking at things. A more paradoxical, and yet coherent, way.

The divine is in humanity. There isn't this big separation of God over here, sacred over here, good over here, and then humans over here, secular over here, bad over here. That was, in fact, a thought that some of the letters of the Bible were written to try to correct.

God is in the human. Always has been.

This has all kinds of implications - way more than just some theological arguments (although those are definitely there as well)

1. Humans matter. A ton. Jesus told humans that they will do greater things than he did. Greater. Greater than Jesus. How would be that be possible? Because the divine is in them.

2. Ceremonies, liturgies, rituals are not magical. They are human. They are your standard flesh and blood (and bread and wine). And that's why they are powerful. We see the divine in the normal and ordinary, especially when we stop and look.

Marriage ceremonies, baptisms, eucharist... nothing happens... except the most powerful thing that can happen... if we see it.

3. Everything is ordinary and yet, completely unordinary, because the Divine lives in the ordinary and the Divine is unordinary ordinary.

4. God will not take care of things. God needs a body. Jesus said this pretty explicitly. When we pray that our friend will somehow get groceries, we remember to go and get those groceries. When we pray for our enemies, we remember to go and be with our

enemies and do good things for them.

When we get mad that God is not solving the refugee crisis we remember that God says something to the effect of... you're right, you have not done anything.

5. The Bible is a human book. Soaked in humanity. And within its culture, context, language, and evolution, we find it soaked in the divine.

This idea may be the biggest foundational reasons I have fallen in love with spirituality again. I began to trust people again, I began to have an optimism about people and God again, I began to see God, be aware of God, wake up to the divine, and I began to feel worthy and accepted and empowered.

All of that just drinking a cup of coffee.

Because I matter. Because you matter. Because they matter. (Every single "they" I can come up with.) Because humans matter.

Because this moment matters.

Because God is all over all of us and it.

Was Jesus fully human? Yes. And God is that.

Leon Dufour a world renowned Jesuit said, "I have written in so many books on God, but after all that, what do I really know? I think, in the end, God is the person you're talking to, the one right in front of you."

If you know that, nothing will ever be the same.

014

just paradox.

Alright, so none of this really makes sense. Not like that.

And, I think, that makes perfect sense to me.

This kind of logic - or lack thereof - can drive people crazy... or to freedom.

To be perfect, you have to stop trying to be perfect.

To know anything, you have to admit you know nothing.

From dust we have come and dust we go, and we are the center of the universe.

The most sacred things are the most ordinary because the sacred is most contained in the ordinary.

Only when we doubt can we have faith.

The questions are more important than the answers.

In dying we live.

In surrendering everything, we find everything.

You yourself are not it. And yet, you are it.

The most powerful thing in all the world is to give up power.

Of course God can't make sense either, right?

And then we have freedom.

015

the angry god.

I used to really love the angry god, because I loved to be angry. I mean if god is angry and I'm supposed to be like God, well... that's a great fit, right? Fun times. I get to be angry and I get to be like god… all at the same time.

I think the angry god is generally the god of angry people.

Others call this god the lifeguard god or the mafia god or the bad parent god and those are not meant as compliments. But, again, if they permit - or, even better, demand - us to be the lifeguards, the mafia, or the parents of the world, well that feels pretty good.

As long as the boss doesn't come after you, of course.

Others call this the god of justice and that is meant as a compliment although I don't take it as one. I mean if someone asked a friend of mine what I was like and they said, "Ryan? Oh he's, a man of justice." I don't think anyone would want to hang out with me. I wouldn't want to.

That god, or type of god, also seems to contradict everything I know about transformation and how it works. So, I don't believe in that god anymore. I think god is always about transformation - the kind of transformation that happens when people realize that the love being offered by the god in question doesn't depend on their transformation.

All of that said, I do think there are some things that get god upset or even angry. (Please remember when I use the word god, I might not be talking about the god you think.) I do think there are some things that get the divine force of good in the universe upset, sometimes even to the point of tears. There are quite a few anger inducing qualifications in the Bible and most of those that matter, can be boiled down to one ingredient: inequality.

When you start looking, it seems like just about all of the anger of God comes back to that word and concept. Inequality, of course, can mean many things but I'm speaking about the perceived value of a human being. Seeing a human as not as worthy, or more worthy, in comparison to another human being is the root of inequality.

Oppression, slavery, racism, sexism, unfair wages... or even viewing yourself as more human than ISIS or a pedophile... one can make a long list of things that center around inequality of one kind or another.

Inequality has all kinds of ripples... and these are where the manifestations of a wrong view of the world start to make trouble. Inequality initiates ladders. If some people are worth more than others, there is a top. If there is a top to the ladder, top to the pyramid, top to whatever structure or system it is than we will all be fighting for that top.

If we have pyramids/ladders/structures, we are going to need some people to make bricks for the pyramid. And, generally, since making bricks is terrible work (no offense masonry workers - I'm talking about historically) we get the slaves to make bricks.

The less thans.

No better way to get to the top than to start some people

working on the very thing you are trying to climb.

Once we have pyramids and ladder and brick makers, we have fear - fear I'll never get to the top (or at least higher than my current location) and fear I'll lose my spot if I do get up there, and someone else will take it from below - mainly those brick makers.

Once we have fear, we have violence... to cover and hide and protect... all those fears. We will do what it takes to get higher or protect our spot. (Violence doesn't always mean blood and guns. The Big Short is one of the most violent movies ever and it's about the housing collapse and big banks killing humanity in all kinds of metaphorical ways).

All of this leads to a further commodification of people, of industry, of anything we need to get up or stay up or not go down.

We have shame, we have ego, we have other gods, we have sacrifices to those gods, we have judgment, we have addiction, we have hypocrisy, we have all kinds of things to try to convince us that we matter more, and they matter less so that we can get higher and stop being lower.

We have blessed and sacred mafia and police and parents and justice, in the name of a god.

The God I believe in isn't down with some people being perceived as less worthy, valued, empowered, and loved than others. And most of the prophets could be summed up with that. I include Jesus with the prophets as well.

I agree that God hates sin... God hates the barriers to equality. (Check out Jubilee, for example. Every 50 years, in Jewish culture, the Monopoly board was reset. Everything was re-distributed equally, debt erased.)

I think this is why Jesus said that someone with lots of money will have a hard time perceiving the world as God does. Money tends to hi-light, enable, and value inequality.

The Divine is never down with someone being seen as less than. And, in that case, God is all about justice. It's never just to view someone as less.

The Divine in us shouldn't be down with inequality either, in any form, no matter how good it makes our ego feel. As good as our ego feels, is as suppressed as the Divine in us feels.

016

at least look down.

An absence of any ladders/pyramids would be ideal. But before we get there, realistically, we should probably acknowledge we're all on them. The ladders of success, of money, of rank, of whatever other word or label we want to put on it.

And most of us are trying to climb.

I'm suggesting we start looking down on our ladders. Actually moving down would be even better, but at least we can start looking down.

Looking up has some serious issues.

For one, we're just looking at people's backs. We just see asses. We start to think the world is filled with asses and we become an ass ourselves. No human can stand looking up at all those asses above us, without becoming one ourself.

You know, you've met that person. Or been that person. Bitter, cynical, sarcastic... muttering how the world is filled with a bunch of greedy, selfish, bastards... because it's all we see as we struggle to push them aside and get higher.

If, however, we decide to look down, it's a very different view. We see faces. We see hands reaching out for our help. We start to realize that there are faces behind all those asses and we start to realize that we've come a lot further than we think and what's the point of trying to climb higher when we can reach out our own hand and try to pull someone up instead.

We'll suddenly be grateful instead of jealous.

We'll suddenly be generous instead of anxious.

We'll suddenly find the world, and life, to generally be a better place.

(Side note: If someone in your life is using you to get higher, they are not a friend. If they are jealous of your spot or anxious of their own, they are also not a friend. They are an equally valuable human, but not a friend.)

The more we look down and pull others up, the less we start to care about the ladders at all. They, conceivably, could even end up collapsing.

I think when Jesus told the rich man to go and sell all his possessions, he was just saying this: go down the ladder. Life is better there.

The man went away sad because he had so much. It's hard to go down the ladder when we're so high up it.

017

pride isn't about you.

Oh man, I was one of the most arrogant people around. I once had a co-worker tell me that it was a good thing that I wasn't good at fighting, because I just had this look of arrogance on me all the time. The look was somewhat intimidating. I loved to argue and I loved to be right.

What an act... Always out to prove something... to someone... mainly myself.

I don't think most humans appreciate arrogance in another human.

But, at the same time, there's confidence. We see it in others and it's so appealing and beautiful. It's not arrogant - there's nothing to prove -but it's so... content with what exists. It's free!

The balance of those is sometimes difficult, especially when we try to address them the wrong way.

We've got to think better of ourselves. The reason I acted arrogant was because I wasn't confident enough. We all know this. It always starts with enough.

Once we think of ourselves as the center of the universe and properly loved and worthy, many will start to sound alarms of pride and/or arrogance, often in Christian circles.

They always did to me.

Don't you know you're supposed to give up your life and serve? You can't think so highly of yourself!

I don't think that's the problem. I never think that thinking the world of yourself is a problem. Unless you think you're the only one in the world.

I think the problem comes when we don't view everyone else as the center of the universe and properly loved and worthy... the exact same as us. That was definitely my problem.

Once we get the value of ourselves as amazing, powerful, incredible and awesome humans (confidence), we shouldn't spend time trying to undo that or listen to any religion that tells us to.

We need to spend time trying to get our worst enemy up to that same spot, not lowering ourselves to them.

Really, once you realize how enough you are, pride has nothing to do with you and everything to do with everyone around you. (In more ways than one.)

018

instead of hate the sinner love the sin...

Love the God in every human
hate anything that blocks you, or them,
from seeing God
and realizing who they are
and what they are capable of.

That's all sin is anyway.

019

god is everywhere except there.

This came from Dave, a friend I always have very deep, paradoxical, confusing and fun conversations with. I gave Dave the "best heretic" award at our church's five year anniversary party because of our conversations.

This, in a nutshell, is one of our conversations:

God is everywhere,
except in the places that we refuse to acknowledge God is.

Of course, God is actually there
but if God is there and we don't care,
is God really there?

God exists in the acknowledgment or awareness of God.

In a sense,
we control where God exists,
because God (and love) allow us to.

So maybe the atheist and the theist are both correct in their reality.

Maybe instead of trying to correct reality, we should seek to acknowledge another reality.

020

that power.

There is the power of dropping bombs
and there is the power of a painting.

There is the power of a jet engine
and there is the power of a melody.

What kind of all-powerful is your god?

This seems like a very important question.

One of my favorites stories might help with an answer.

Many years ago, in a far away land, there had been a drought for a long time and, of course, the gods were being blamed, as they often were. And are. The king of the land worshiped a god of rain and he was convinced that his god was not the problem, this time... but that another god was the problem. The god of a prophet.

So, the prophet and the king agreed, in the only way that makes sense, to a battle of the gods to see which god was more powerful and to determine who was to blame for the drought and famine that was killing the land.

Was it the god of the king or the god of the prophet?

The king had his own prophets - around 450 of them - show up at the event. I imagine flags and trumpets and spectacle. The goal of the competition was to bring down some fire - to prove which god was more powerful. (Again, if you're going to have your gods do something - bringing down fire seems pretty cool.)

In the story, the 450 prophets of the king, after a lot of drama, aren't able to get their god to do anything. No fire. No anything really. It's not going well for them.

The prophet of the other god, ever the performer and antagonizer, then asks everyone to make the challenge a little more difficult - just to prove a point - before asking his god to send down fire to consume a bull, now surrounded by water, that had been set up.

Fire comes from heaven. Drama. Power. Slam dunk. Home run.

Drop the mic. Challenge over. The god of the prophet wins.

The prophet looks at the king and says maybe my favorite line of any story, "Go, eat and drink, for there is the sound of heavy rain."

Boom.

The prophet then finds himself on the run, scared for his life.

I can't say that's what I was expecting the first time I read the story. Not the normal thing course of action after your god beats the other god.

The prophet finds himself out in the wilderness for 40 days. (By the way, tons of stories have 40: the Hebrew people were in the wilderness 40 years, Noah was on a boat while it rained for 40 days, Moses was on Mt. Sinai for 40 days, Jonah warned Nineveh for 40 days, and Jesus was in the wilderness 40 days and after the resurrection was on Earth for 40 days. According to the rabbis, 40 represents transition or change.)

Apparently the challenge and battle of the gods didn't really work.

The "winner" is out in the desert, changing, while the "loser" is eating bread and drinking wine in his castle. Interesting.

Around this 40 day (transition) point, the prophet's god comes by and asks him what he is doing there. Interesting question. I would have answered "running for my life because of you." The prophet didn't.

The god then says go up to a mountain - I'm going to pass by.

The story then says there were earthquakes, more fire, and wind. All very powerful things. But, the story tells us that the god was not in any of those powerful things.

There was, however, a gentle whisper. That's where God was, the story insists. In the whisper. After fire and earthquakes and wind. I wonder if those 40 days made the prophet change, transition or evolve his views on where the power of his god actually was.

Generations later, the disciples of Jesus were hanging out and getting really upset at a group of people that they already generally hated (and found to be ignorant and wrong and stupid). That same group had not welcomed them and accepted their message. So, obviously, they asked Jesus if they should call down fire on the village just like the prophet in the story had. (Before we get all high and mighty, most people still ask their god to send down fire on their enemies. Or at least bless the fire of their bombs and missiles.) And Jesus turns and rebukes them, and says, quite astoundingly, you don't know what spirit you are talking about here...

There were not that many spirits to choose from in that worldview - spirits from god (the source of all good) and spirits from the devil (the source of all evil).

Which kind of all-powerful is the god of the Bible?

It would seem to not be the power of bombs, of jet engines, of judges handing out verdicts, of fire, of earthquakes, of the things that rattle the windows of our souls with fear, but instead...

more like the power of paintings, songs, stories of grace and tenderness, laying down, resting, and quiet whispers that soften our souls with love.

That's the kind of power that changes humanity for the better.

That's Godly power.

021

silence.

I recently found myself on a long run in a time of a lot of stress. The run ended up feeling like I imagine Native American teenagers felt as they searched to find their spirit animal. I know I hadn't smoked anything but, at times I felt like I had.

My only goal in starting the run was to listen. I promised myself to simply listen to everything that came my way.

Amazingly enough, as soon as I left my house a little girl (in the middle of the day - I'm still not sure what she was doing out there alone) said "hello" to me. It was as though the world was saying "Welcome, Ryan".

It was difficult at first. I wanted to think and solve and forecast the future so I could think and solve imaginary problems too. But then I kept saying "listen". Listen to my feet, to birds, to cars, to my breathing.

I found myself running my some lions in cages. (We have a zoo called Cat Tales not far from my house. It's filled with lions, tigers, and other felines.) I noticed that the animals were making noises as they pranced around their cages and I noticed that the humans in their houses were making similar noises across the street as they pounced around in their caged yards.

Where is all the promised freedom, I asked. I kept running and listening. Which I soon noticed I do a lot. I keep running. From whatever it is.

So, I stopped running and listened more intently. After every stop I found myself running with more energy and inspiration. Another lesson.

Then I realized I always run the same path. So I started running on different paths, on different roads, on hills. At one point I stopped at the top of a hill, listening for a while and raised my hands in the air as though I had just won a race. I was either crazy or symbolically expressing what stopping and listening is: it's winning.

I don't know how far I ran or how I long. I know I kept listening. Whenever stress came, I listened. I ran by some cows and they all yelled at me. Maybe they were simply saying hi or maybe they were saying hey, we feel you man. It's good to listen and we hope you're enjoying it. Life is better when you do.

By the time I came home, I was overwhelmed with silence. The overwhelming sense of stress and solving and planning and finding solutions and running was silenced by silence.

By just listening. Literally and metaphorically and spiritually.

It's called noise pollution. It's everywhere. Our machines alter environments not just visibly but audibly. Our noise, like the cars I heard, drastically affect animals and ecosystems. Our noise alone changes our world.

John Cage wrote the song 4'33" in 1952. During the first performance of the song David Tudor opens his piano and sits there for 30 seconds. He then closes the piano, opens it again and sits there for 2 minutes and 23 seconds. He then closes and opens again for a final 1 minute and 40 seconds. The song is 4 minutes and 33 seconds of silence.

Of course there are all kinds of jokes and ridicule about the "song" and its ridiculousness and absurdity.

Yves Klein showcased an art exhibit of blank walls at the Galerie

Iris Clert in Paris in 1958. There was literally nothing there but blank white walls. The Pompideu in Paris recently duplicated the exhibit.

Again the laughs of art history professors everywhere. (I'm hearing by art history professor brother right now and I know this kind of stuff drives him crazy.)

But, let's step back for a second.

Elizabeth Gilbert says 4 words profoundly changed her life: "shut the fuck up." She realized that her parents were not asking her for all of her great advice on their marriage and that, unless they asked, she should simply remain silent.

Speaking wouldn't change them anyway.

This epiphany extended far beyond her parents. Why do we insist on speaking to people who are not asking for our opinion?

Every time I go on Facebook now, I can't help but think of that f in the logo as a giant symbol of shut the f up. Facebook is perhaps one of the greatest noise pollutants in our society (no offense Mark).

What kind of things would your hear and notice if you had to sit still for 4 minutes and 33 seconds?

What kind of things would you begin to think of if you entered into an empty room for a few moments?

Be quiet. Just listen. Listen to God, the Universe, the Divine, or whatever other name you want to put on the power that is rolling through it and you and everyone around you. Listen to it. Pay attention. Paying attention is prayer.

Listen to the Earth. To the birds, to water, to air rushing through your windows, to rain, to the leaves rustling and to the vastness of space.

Listen to others. They have amazing stories. They are invaluable as contributors to this planet, humanity, and your own story.

Listen to what they have to teach you. Even your biggest adversary. The one who disagrees with you the most. What do you learn about yourself when you stop and listen?

Harriet Lerner, via Brené Brown says, “Change requires listening with the same level of passion that we feel when we speak.”

Listen to yourself. The divine dwells in you. Your body is speaking. Your mind is speaking. Your soul is speaking if you just listen.

It’s a loud world. Find quiet and space to breathe, to contemplate and to just listen.

If continued evolution, growth, adaptation is our point, listening might be one of the most powerful things on Earth.

022

enough more.

I'll be honest, I struggle with these words and I don't think I'm the only one.

How do I be grateful for what I have?
And still want more?

How do I be content with the way things are?
And still push for better and bigger?

How do I live in the now?
And dream about a brighter future?

How do I continue to evolve?
And appreciate where I'm at.

I'm always nervous to boil things down too much but, it seems, at the end of the day, there are two approaches we can take:

we can pursue more to get to enough.
we can realize enough and pursue more out of that.

The first is generally the way our economy and culture functions and it wants it that way because it makes a lot of money for a lot of people: Keep getting more and someday you will have enough. There is little talk about what "enough" actually looks like because, in that model, "enough" doesn't actually exist. There is always more to get. And enough is always in the future meaning that more never stops... more shoes, more shirts, more apps, more knowledge, more songs, more articles...

Not to get too political here, but in a capitalistic system there is never enough. Otherwise the system would crumble.

There are also some religious cultures that prefers this way of living. Religious production and consumption benefits many people in religious power. You need to do more, to get to enough and the people who are providing more and determining enough are very powerful and in control. The never-ending desire to be enough (thus attaining more) is just where they want people. Religious capitalism.

The second concept is different.

How do I pursue an awareness that I am enough?

How do you pursue an awareness that you are enough?

How do we really live in a world of enough?

Enough money, enough awards, enough prestige, enough power, enough worth, enough...

Once we have thoroughly understood enough, experienced enough, and lived enough... more appears and moves very differently. And when it does it's usually more generosity, more joy, more patience, more color, more calm, more giving, more rest, more creativity, more diversity, more experiences, and more love.

The Jesuits call this the "magis". The first time I heard about the "magis" I almost started crying because it was the first time I felt pursuing more was okay. Magis is Latin for "more".

James Martin writes that "the magis means doing the more, the greater, for God. When you work, give your all, When you make plans, plan boldly. And when you dream, dream big... Ultimately, 'eliciting great desires' and inviting people to think big is the seed for accomplishing great things for God."

There is a pursuit of more that is absolutely beautiful and inspiring... scientists say that Dark Energy - that thing that makes up a huge percentage of our universe that we don't really know what it is - contains the universe and propels it forward.

Contains and propels.

We can't propel to find containment. We have to realize we are contained and then propel as contained beings.

Mixing up our pursuit of more and our pursuit of enough can be exhausting, debilitating, and even deadly. I see it constantly. I've lived it.

Again, you are enough. Right now.
Get that, and then get more.
Don't try to get more to get that.

Seek first the Kingdom of God (and its perspective on the world) and everything else will come when it should, is how, I believe, Jesus worded it.

023

enough is hard.

Yeah, yeah, we hear it and you've heard it. But seriously, this enough stuff. Can anyone actually live it? Can anyone actually go through life believing and living "enough"?

This is so frustrating. We resist the most, that which makes us a better person. I know I do, at least.

Not because we don't want to be better people. I know I do.

But because to be better we have to give up the struggle to be enough and we have to realize we are and we have to

be naked and vulnerable
risk the most important thing we think we own - our own merit and worth
give up control of the things we think we control
say no to the comforting, intoxicating whisper of the ego and its power and
acknowledge mystery and doubt and admit we don't know more than we think we know.

You have to lose your life to find it.

024

you are.

When I made video games for a living, my boss gave me an Eeyore to hold my business cards. I was grumpy, pessimistic, negative... I was Eeyore.

And then something happened, and that something had a lot to do with faith and God and Christianity. I don't want to say it was solely responsible but it's amazing how often a bad faith story will affect the rest of someone's life story and perspective.

I found a faith that said to celebrate more. Be proud of myself more. Acknowledge that I've grown, evolved, that I'm learning, that I've failed - and learned from that - and that I am moving. At least a little. I know I have. And you have. Everyone has. But negative thoughts stick to our brain much more easily than positive. You have to work to make those positive thoughts stick.

Instead of focusing on all the things that you have not done correctly, (often for which you think God is about to roast you) start focusing on the good things you are doing. Focus on how proud God is of you. Focus on how proud you are of yourself. Focus on how often you can relate to people trying to figure out life.

Sometimes you feed the hungry, clothe the naked, and visit the sick. You reject money for something more important. You take time to rest and breathe and appreciate the moment.

And on and on it goes. Religion is often just affirming that the things that feel like they bring you life, actually are.

So be grateful, pat yourself on the back and smile.

025

pick your run.

We can run one of three ways.

Many people feel like they are running from something. The monster is chasing them.

They are fleeing from Hell. From regret. From shame. From punishment. On and on the list goes, but whenever we are running from something, we are in living in a place of fear.

Many people are running toward something. The reward is in front of them.

Toward grace. Toward freedom. Toward reward. Toward enough. Toward love. On and on the list goes, but whenever we are running toward something, we are living in a place of love.

There's not a scary, falling apart, going-to-Hell world out there that we need to run away from. There's a big beautiful world full of humans that we are called to run full speed ahead into, anticipating big beautiful things.

Many people are running in the moment. Just aware of what is happening around them.

We can still run to something and be aware of what's around us. It's much more difficult to run from something and be aware of what's around us. There's too much fear and adrenaline and panic.

Run to.

See now.

Run to.

026

ordinary is not.

First, if you have never read *Tattoos on the Heart* by Father Greg Boyle (Father G) maybe you should stop reading this book and read that one and then come back to this. It's life-changing.

Father G says: "The incarnation is not that we forget the eucharist is sacred - it's that we forget it's ordinary."

Denise Scott Brown, the architect, says "Basically, the idea is that with everyone striving to be revolutionary, you will be most revolutionary if you try to be ordinary."

That was not the way my thinking generally went for years. Someone recently asked me how I was doing spiritually. When I told them I was doing great spiritually because I've realized that there is no "spiritual" part of my life, I realized how much I've changed.

Our biggest danger is not that we might forget that there are sacred things in this world, it's that we might forget that there are only sacred things.

That piece of fruit.
That kiss.
That feeling of the keyboard against your fingertips.
Those blades of grass swaying in the breeze.
The homeless vet with the cardboard sign.
The bored moments.

They are all sacred spaces because there are no ordinary spaces or people or actions.

That, truly, changes everything. It has changed things for me more than any other single concept or thought or idea.

027

operating systems.

With all this talk of evolution and change and adapting, maybe it's a good spot to compare it to something else, always changing:

Operating systems.

With every new operating system release, the same kind of things happen. It doesn't matter whether the operating system is Android, Mac OS, Windows, or simply a change in websites...

Some complain that it's more confusing.
Some complain that they liked the old one better.
Some don't understand the new functionality.
Some don't understand why they changed it again.
Some try to learn.
Some love it.
Some can't believe how much better it is.
Some can't imagine how they ever did work in the old one.

No matter the response, if someone doesn't keep up on the iterations, at some point, they will not be able to use the machine. Unfortunately, it's often the elderly at the butt of these jokes. It moved too fast and they haven't kept up. They're now lost.

Then, inevitably, the talk of a time when we didn't need that specific machine begins... to make ourselves feel better for not being able to operate the machine in question.

When I grew up no one had a computer! How ridiculous!

But the universe keeps putting out new operating systems because that's what the universe does. It moves. It advances. It evolves whether we like it or not. The driving force of the universe is a little new, then some more new, and then a sprinkle and dash of a little more new and then a lot of new just to pile on the new that we haven't quite caught up with yet.

By default, that means there are constant mysteries, unknowns, uncertainty, and new operating systems to make us look stupid. As the Italian theoretical physicist Carlo Rovelli puts it "It is hardly surprising that there are more things in heaven and earth, dear reader, than have been dreamed of in our philosophy— or in our physics. We did not even suspect the existence of radio waves and neutrinos, which fill the universe, until recently."

Science gets this. They are fine being found stupid - in fact it means that something new has been discovered. Stupidity is almost celebrated. Mystery and searching demands admitting some stupidity.

Religion is the same. There is always new. Some religious followers insist that we have figured out everything because somewhere along the lines mixing religion and stupidity was dangerous - but that is like a scientist insisting that Newton was correct in the way he saw the universe. You'd be laughed out of the building.

Religion, to keep up with this universe (and God) is no different. It has to evolve. It's got to move. It can't sit still or it becomes useless... and one of my favorite things about Christianity is that it has done exactly that. This is not a knock, this is a gift.

I assume we are somewhere around Christianity version 43174.3 at this point. Roughly.

And like all updates, there are many who say they don't understand the language. It's confusing. They liked the old one better. They don't understand the new functionality or why it was changed. Others embrace it and try to keep learning and can't believe how much bigger and better it is.

These trends tend to stick with generations.

The Macintosh operating system is now over 30 years old. The first iteration looks nothing like the most recent one.. and yet it does. It works the same basic way. It was built on it. It wouldn't exist without it. It's so new and yet, so not.

For those who want to go back to the old operating system, there are no current machines that run it. No software. No capability to do anything. And if you were to insist on using an old machine, you would be missing out on so much.

And to say that Apple is no longer the creators of the new operating system because it's so different than the first one... that would be ignorant and foolish. And to imply that Apple was so content with their original creation that they became something other than Apple, is equally ignorant. Apple thinks differently. Apple creates. It's who they are.

They can't stop.

I hope Apple is not more creative than the creative force behind all creativity. That would seem a little strange. To quote Pope Francis, "God is not afraid of new things."

To add to it, God insists on new operating systems.

028

re-moving.

It also might be useful, at this point, to give an illustration on two ways to look at human beings and their interaction with the divine. It could be helpful to be a little more blunt on some Christian perspectives and language on the world...

I did this as a sermon and I was shocked at the response. I thought I had been saying this all along but sometimes you just need to spell it out.

Example one: Bulb World.

Imagine a light. The light is not turned on but the bulb is sitting there. Many people live in a world where their religious job is to turn on the light in people. They come, tell them a story of a god, a prophet, or a way to live, the person believes that story and the light comes on. (Now, of course, there is all kinds of language and disagreement about who actually turns the light on but that doesn't really matter.) The light needs to be turned on. Missionaries went to Brazil to turn on the lights. To bring something that was not there. To accomplish a divine mission.

Well mission accomplished. Once the person says a prayer, gets dunked, or whatever sign indicates that the light is on, the person whose job it is to turn on lights can move on to the next bulb that has not yet been "activated".

If the person is starving, that is unfortunate, but at least the light has now been turned on and eternal salvation awaits! After they starve to death, but still.

Example two: Light World.

Imagine the same light. This time it is on and shining brightly. In fact, it's shining in everyone. All humans are already lit. The lights are burning bright.

However, it's not all "as it should be". There are dark blankets covering up those lights. Hiding them from ourselves, from others, from the world. We do all kinds of things to cover up those lights. We cover them in shame, in "sin", in violence, in ego, in jealousy, addiction, materialism, fear, and on and on it goes.

In this perspective, no one has the job of turning on the light, but we all have the job of removing dark things that are blocking the light. (With this in mind, I'm definitely cool with Jesus "dying for our sins". Jesus died for all the crap that covers the light inside of us including a sacrificial system based on shame and violence in the hopes of becoming "enough".)

In this case, the mission does change.

Feeding someone removes something covering the light. Relieving someone of addictive behavior can remove a layer that is covering the light. There are all kinds of ways to remove the layers that block that light and these things are divine and sacred and powerful and "missionary". When Jesus talked about feeding people and feeding him, I don't think he meant that literally but he did mean there was something in him that's in them.

The mystics, for what it's worth, have generally seen things more like example two - I also include Jesus in this category. He did say he came to help the blind "see" and I don't think he meant that literally.

With example two, spirituality becomes more about subtraction - not addition. It becomes more about becoming aware of what is real and removing the things that hide that reality. It becomes more about helping others to do the same thing. I've got nothing to bring, that isn't already there.

Interestingly enough, athletes will often speak in a similar manner - what makes them great is their ability to focus on what is important and to ignore the distraction, the irrelevant, and unnecessary information.

There is a lot of distraction, irrelevant and unnecessary information in religion today that, I think, should be ignored in order to enable us to focus on what is actually important.

Seeing who we are and what we are capable of.

029

ego.

I was headed to a meeting last week and I had a talk with my ego. This is not something I've done until recently, but I'm doing more.

I address my ego by name. I looked over at the seat. "Rhino," I said. (That's my ego's name.)

"I love you. You are the man. You are awesome. I appreciate you for everything you do. You have helped to shape me into who I am today. But, right now, I don't need you to come this meeting with me. In fact, I prefer if you stay in the car. I'm going to be good without you! I can handle it. So, I'll see you later."

The ego. Rhino rides through life with me, making me do things I don't want to do. But, I do want to do.

Richard Rohr says that we should change "flesh" in the Bible, especially with Paul, to ego.

I agree. It would make a lot more sense. (Especially when John begins his book with the idea of the Word becoming flesh... and that was apparently pretty awesome. So this flesh stuff is not all bad.)

The ego has done some good for us as we've grown and become who we are. But now, it's mostly damaging. It's that thing that we are all fighting.

I think we can boil it down to the ego and the divine in each of us.

In constant battle.

The ego loves to belittle to make itself feel better.
The divine already knows its the best.

The ego loves to congratulate itself that it's not like them.
The divine already knows we're all the same.

The ego says we earned it.
The divine says it's all a gift.

The ego says they are evil.
The divine says they are children.

They ego loves bad religion.
The divine is repelled by it.

If we really want to know exactly what the ego looks like in human form, we can look at the Pharisees.

If we really want to know exactly what the divine looks like in human form, we can look at Jesus.

They don't get along well at all.

Jesus came to free the ego from its chains but in order to do so, the ego had to acknowledge the audacity of love for everyone.

It couldn't handle it. So it killed the divine.

We've got be careful of the ego. It's still killing the divine in people everywhere. It's still killing the divine in us.

You might want to let it know that you would prefer it didn't.

030

empowerment is often not.

I have good friends who work with refugees, teen moms, ex-convicts, gangs, at-risk youth, people with no homes, and all kinds of other amazing human beings on the fringes of society, trying to fight their way back in. I hear a common thread from all the people working with these people to improve their lives: those on the fringes need jobs.

But, they don't really mean that they just need jobs - we already employ enough human beings on the fringes of society. Sometimes that employment takes advantage of their placement on the fringe. What my friends mean is that these people need to believe they are worth something and that they matter. Jobs often tell them that, tangibly, for the first time.

Jobs give them some hope that they can actually do this.

There is another common thread to refugees, teen moms, ex-convicts, gang members, at-risk youth, people with no homes, and all kinds of other amazing human begins on the fringes of society trying to fight their way back in. They've been told they suck. Over and over in conscious and sub-conscious ways, in intentional and accidental ways, in individual and societal ways. They've heard the message loud and clear, repeatedly from a variety of sources: you are not worth a damn. You're worthless and a piece of shit.

This, of course, has all kinds of implications for all kinds of issues, including, but not limited to prison systems.

Bastoy prison in Norway made the news for its treatment of its prisoners. At Bastoy, prisoners live on an island with no guards, no fences, and no cells. They are given houses, allowances, and told, in a wide variety of ways, they are worth something. (Ironic that all of this happens in a "secular" nation.)

The governor of the prison has said: "If we treat people like animals when they are in prison they are likely to behave like animals. Here we pay attention to you as human beings... They look at themselves in the mirror, and they think, 'I am shit. I don't care. I am nothing,'...This prison, gives them a chance to see they have worth, to discover, 'I'm not such a bad guy.'"

Norway the country has one of the lowest re-offense rates in the world and Bastoy, as a prison, even lower.

All of this comes to empowerment. It's a sexy topic and for good reason: people need to be empowered. They need to get the job, to be treated as a human being, they need to believe that they are not a piece of shit. In fact, they are quite the opposite: pieces of humanity that are precious and whose worth can not be measured.

But much of our "empowerment" is more like treating humans like animals, and sub-consciously telling them they are still worthless. Here's your treat. Here's you food. Here's your shoes. I will take care of you because you can't.

Empowerment movements can be tricky. We need to be careful of the traps of easy empowerment: the kind of empowerment that doesn't empower anyone except the person already in power because they helped someone who couldn't help themselves.

True empowerment requires seeing the world differently. It requires seeing human beings as equal to myself. It requires our time, our effort, our money, our investment, our everything... to assure them that they matter. Way more than they think. They matter as much as ourselves.

It's risky and revolutionary and it requires us to die to our egos… it's painful. But the only way to truly tell someone they have power, is to give up a bit of my own, which might be why I find myself drawn to easy empowerment and nervous of the true.

Talking about equality is easy but living it is pretty hard, because I still don't think most of us believe...

I am enough.

031

eternal fire.

We might have really messed up what we think God wants to destroy. I've heard more people talk about God destroying actual people than God destroying the things that prevent people from actually seeing who they are.

I think that's the stuff that is more important to God to start burning: anything that prevents us from living in the light and realizing what we are.

John the Baptist was out in the desert talking about unquenchable fires that burn up chaff. I once saw this verse on a billboard warning people of the fire that was coming to get them.

Ironically, Luke, in that passage, called the fire, along with some other words, good news.

When was the last time unquenchable fire was good news? More often than not, the unquenchable fire that we hear about is the main feature of the bad news that is supposedly why we need the good news - to save us from that fire.

That's messed up.

This fire is great news. It's burning up ego, boxes, shame and all the other things (sin) that prevent us from living and being what we are.

If there is fire, I hope it's burning up that stuff. Forever.

032

new labels.

I was just talking to a family who lives in Egypt and our conversation, honestly, got really messed up when we insisted on using the words “Muslim” and “Christian”.

Muslims think this about Christians. (What kind of Muslims? What kind of Christians?)

And the Christians (what kind?) act so weird toward the Muslims (which ones?) that...

I just don’t find any of the conversations about those words fascinating anymore. Or not as fascinating as words like extremists, fundamentalists, agnostics, apathetic, and liberated. Those seem more valuable.

To get even more simple, and follow Anthony DeMello’s lead, what if we just talked about humanity in terms of those who live in places of fear and those who live in places of love?

Anger, hate, resentment, vengeance, violence, shame, criticism, and the like seem to live in the land of fear.

Contentedness, grace, breathing, accepting, awareness, trust, generosity, and the like seem to live in the land of love.

It’s about love and fear. When it’s about that, the entire conversation becomes more interesting, helpful, inspiring, persuasive, and productive, and then we can talk about what kind of Atheists, Christians and Muslims we are and what those words mean to us.

Where do you live? Where does your faith pitch a tent? Where does your religion build a temple? In the land of fear or the land of love?

That's a fascinating conversation.

033

you can't go home.

Everything about this universe is expanding. And those who know, I trust, now tell us that it's increasing in its expansion. And those who know, I trust, now tell us that the expansion is increasing faster than we thought!

I could go into all the details - and others have at various times - but here's the gist as I understand it: The place we live, the things we're made of, surrounded by, sustained by, the cycles, the systems, the, everything, is getting bigger.

Because, if you read the story of the Bible as a big story, which we sometimes forget it is, it's a story of people getting bigger. Of growing in their understanding of God, their tribe, of each other, of themselves, of the universe...

If you look at Jesus, Jesus came to keep the momentum, and more than likely, increase it toward bigger. Yeah you thought you shouldn't include them, I do. You thought you shouldn't believe that, I do. You thought God was in that box, no. You thought you had it all figured out, you don't.

This is, and always has been, about getting bigger. Expanding our views, our experiences, our hearts, our souls, our love.

There is bigger and there is home. And, as much as home sounds great - I mean it is safe and known and certain - if you've ever moved, like I have, you find something really interesting about home. And this has become a cliché because so many have experienced it.

It's so small. You go back and visit the camp, the house, the backyard, the pool, the amusement park that seemed so overwhelmingly large, and, after you've grown, it seems so small and, tiny, and almost claustrophobic.

The goal is childlike - as grown adults. Children are constantly changing... learning, asking, seeking, adapting.

But you can't go back to the places you once lived. Home was great and got you to this point. But you're grown up now. Paul said something similar when he talked about the fact that we aren't children anymore and therefore should be happy with what that means - we do live a little differently. The walls and boxes and rules that once offered safety, now offer stagnation and incarceration.

There is a common thread among fundamentalists of every kind: they want to go home. Home was safe, home was comfortable, home was where it was good.

Besides things like hindsight bias, which make us always remember the past as better than it was - because we've now lived through it and seen that we make it - there is something else about the past...

It doesn't exist.

It's no longer that home. That place. That sidewalk and tree and you. Those who insist on going back and taking the world with them will find it very frustrating. Fundamentalism is always frustrating.

It's not the movement of the universe.

034

the other side.

Jesus returns from the dead and starts making breakfast on a beach. The disciples are out fishing and aren't aware that Jesus is around yet. (Is there a better illustration of resurrection ever?)

These disciples are having bad luck catching anything and Jesus tells them to try the other side of the boat.

Interesting. Had they not thought of that, already? Did they always fish on one side? Was that the lucky side? The easy side? The good side? Are different sides of boats really that different?

They suddenly catch a ton of fish. It's a miracle!

And they know it's Jesus.

I'm not sure this really has anything to do with fishing. I think it has to do with ruts. It's easy to get stuck in them. It's easy to think it's not working but we just need to keep trying harder and more and doing the same thing over and over.

Then someone come along and says try the other side of the boat. Try something new. Different. Get out of the rut.

God doesn't like ruts. There are no fish there. Or miracles.

Again, it's time to try the new.

035

the devil gets all the good ones.

About a year ago, I had the privilege of hearing the story of Amanda Lindhout. To make a long (amazing) story short, Amanda traveled to Somalia "the most dangerous place on earth," to photograph and learn more about those affected by wars, famine, and drought.

She was kidnapped after a short time and spent 460 days in captivity.

While in captivity she was abused in every way imaginable and somehow found a way to forgive her captives while they abused her, to find empathy for their story, while their story affected her own in traumatic and devastating ways. Mind-blowing forgiveness. There is not a person I tell the story to who doesn't sit in awe for a moment. As I heard her speak, I was in awe myself.

She also told her story of an attempted escape. Her and her fellow captive managed to get to a mosque. Unfortunately, her captors eventually found her as well but she tells the story of an older woman who literally laid down on her body in order to try and prevent her captives from re-taking her. The woman screamed and yelled and did everything she could for this white stranger, risking her own life. The last image Amanda saw of this mystery woman she was lying on the floor of the mosque, with tears, reaching out her own hands to try to reach her.

The story was maybe the most powerful I've ever heard. Gorgeous. Inspiring and humbling.

Amanda has since returned to Somalia numerous times to continue to try and help the people there and continue her own path of replacing anger with grace.

At the end of the story, I remember a friend of mine looking at me and saying, "Amazing story. Too bad that Muslim woman and Amanda are going to Hell" because they aren't Christians.

She was being sarcastic. (I'm really trying to be less sarcastic but man, I joined in on that one.)

Another friend added, "Isn't it too bad the devil gets all the good ones?"

I mean, honestly, doesn't it seem that way sometimes with certain religious world views?

There are, apparently, so many good people, saving the world, laying down their life for others, who haven't said a prayer, and so many people who have said a prayer, waiting on their couch for the world to end in doom and destruction and the second group keep saying it's not about "being good".

If I was being sarcastic I might say... well that's great that you have a nice little saying to make you feel better while you sit on that couch.

Jesus talked about feeding people, visiting them in jail, and, not to put words in his mouth, but laying down your life for strangers in a mosque and forgiving someone as they are physically assaulting you.

And it wasn't about action. That just gets us back to doing more. It was about a perspective and attitude and awareness that enables us to do those things for our fellow humans and for the divine because we are drawn to both of them all around us.

When you have that, at least in the story of the sheep and goats,

God says come on in to a world that is much better than you anticipate. When you don't, God says away from me. I, the divine, don't live in the world where you refuse to recognize it in everyone.

036

who loves more?

Three days after the shooting in Charleston, North Carolina, families of the victims were asking for God to show mercy to the shooter.

Three days after people lost a close family member because someone generally didn't like any people of their family members' color and attended a Bible Study with those people in order to be warmly accepted by them and then shoot them... the family members offered them forgiveness and grace.

And many would say that God is sending that shooter to Hell, unable to offer the same grace.

Are people more loving than God?

If that is true, than it seems like we have a major problem with God. It can't be possible that the created beings love more than the Creator, right?

If that isn't true, than I think we have a major problem with Hell.

I do tend to side with the second.

Mark Twain once asked "Who prays for Satan... the one sinner that needed it most...".

Crazy enough, I learned the answer to that: the Athonite monks of Cyprus. They actually pray for the demons and the devil on a regular basis - to find salvation and God.

Once again, if there are human beings praying for the devil to be saved… I wonder if God feels the same way?

I know we have a major problem with Hell.

For those that do insist on a Hell and do want people there, I wonder if they are already there. It's a tough life to feel like everyone around you needs to be punished a little bit more than they already are. That can make you really angry.

And, you have to wonder. If someone can not fathom the idea of Hitler being in Heaven, what kind of Heaven would it be for that person if Hitler is there?

It could be pretty hellish.

Or one could say, that God, in God's mercy and justice, develops a place to live for people who can't stand Hitler being in Heaven, and calls it Hell, because God definitely loves humans more than we are capable of.

037

heaven as a perspective.

Pierre Teilhard de Chardin's theme is evolution. He argues, in his amazing book *Christianity and Evolution* that it's our job to evolve. It's the job of the universe to evolve, and it is the job of Christians to push evolution. It's our main mission, he argues.

Pain pushes evolution. It's how we move. de Chardin even argues that we should all celebrate pain because it's then that we are growing. We need pain. Of course, God created pain - it's necessary to evolve and God is all about evolution and growth.

It's all about perspective. Our perspective on failure, perspective on mistakes, perspective on pain.

What if heaven is just a different perspective on pain? What if heaven is not the absence of pain? What if there are no more tears because we realize there is nothing to cry about? What if there is no more sadness because we see sadness for what it actually is?

There is still learning and growing in heaven and there is a reason we can't all just get to Heaven right now - we have to evolve in our understanding of pain a little more.

038

heaven and hell are not different places.

Imagine a room. It's filled with color, with people, with love and with God. It's everything you could hope for. As long as you can see it and experience it and as long as your eyes aren't closed.

The same room, with your eyes closed, or the lights off, is dark, empty, alone and frightening.

I think we need to stop trying to get some place or do something other than open our eyes to what is here. That's what we're supposed to be learning: How to see the world, the trees, the animals, the air, the food, how to see the people in it, those we love and those we hate, and how to see ourselves... with all the color, love and God that is there.

When we learn that, it doesn't matter where we are... it's Heaven.

And, on the flip side, if you're in Heaven with your eyes closed, it will be Hell.

Sadly, many of the people waiting the most for Heaven are only learning how to be unaware of it, when they are there. And thus, they will find themselves in Hell, saying, I thought it would be better than this when I died and everything finally took care of itself.

I can imagine God coming along and saying... oh you're in Heaven alright, but you've got to open your eyes.

And they will say, but how?

And God could say... well, that was how you were created but you just spent 70 years learning how to close them to everything.

That might be why Jesus was so tricky when he talked about the people who would be there (and are there now) and the people who wouldn't (and aren't there now).

It had very little to do with "performing miracles", "casting out demons", and "prophesying" and everything to do with seeing the world, the people in it, and ourselves in a certain… light.

It also had a lot to do with love.

039

love is the hardest thing.

I have heard way too many times, people, especially religious people, speak very derogatory language about love, as though it's so simple and easy and so much more is required of us. They will talk as though people who just try to love are missing the boat and not wanting to get into the "challenging/difficult/real/deep stuff".

People often use this kind of language in trying to be critical of another church (a good sign of not loving in itself). They will say "Yeah they're just a little too love-y for me."

Can we please stop this nonsense?

There is nothing on this planet harder than loving everyone on it and treating them with patience, kindness, and that whole list of things that you want to be treated with and that is read at weddings to define love.

Equally hard is allowing yourself to believe that you are enough, you are worthy, you are just as great without the new clothes, car, partner, book, or whatever else, as you are with it and that God (or the universe or a power greater than you) actually loves you, independent of how cool you are, how great your theology is, or whether or not you have it all figured out.

Love is the most difficult thing.

Which is probably why Jesus knew that he didn't really need to say or do much else.

And they still killed him.

Note: Love also gets people killed fairly often, which means powerful people are deathly afraid of it.

040

violent love.

Violence is around a lot of conversations and for good reason. The world is filled with it. The Bible is filled with it and we're always trying to reconcile our views of grace with justice, of mercy with order, of peace with violence.

Here are some way too simple thoughts.

Love is the absence of fear.

We fear love.

Violence and fear are always related.

Violence can be useful to destroy boxes and cages.

Violence is an excuse for the ego to have full control and that's always dangerous. But, in a sense, love is violent, or can be, but not in the common understanding of violent. But those paradoxes of revolutionary love, rebellious love.. violent love are valid.

If violence is done out of fear... than it's always destructive and harmful.

If there is no fear, then it's love, and actions done without fear can still be tearing, gashing, and almost violent.. but always healing.

Bravery... protecting love... great.
Bravery... protecting fear... not great.

And sometimes it's hard to tell the difference.

Sometimes what some call love others calls violence and what some call violence others call love.

One more thought.

If you're going to justify your own violence as righteous, you have to allow God to be violent as well.

041

heroic.

Why is it generally considered more, courageous, valiant, and heroic to die while trying to kill an enemy than it is to die while trying to love an enemy?

Also, if dying while trying to kill an enemy is heroic, we better be sure we know why ISIS is not heroic.

042

love.

In the late 1960's the New York Subway system had a terrible problem. People were walking around confused as to where to go because the signs were so bad.

The Transit Authority hired Massimo Vignelli and Bob Noorda to solve their problems. And they did. They created the, now famous, New York City Transit Authority Graphic Standards Manual in 1970.

The standard nailed down colors, text, fonts, where to place fonts, and names and subway lines and it's been in use for almost fifty years now.

Lots of people are walking around confused in religion, specifically Christianity, today. They are wandering toward bad signs and trying to figure out God, themselves, others, the Bible, and a host of other things. I'm the first one to raise my hand and say - yep, that's me!

But it seems the signs have been terrible. Or maybe we just ignored the standard that was created: love.

As much as we want to make something more to it, there isn't. It's just love. Period.

We really really really want to add a but to love.

Love, but

they are pedophiles
they are terrorists
they are evil
they need to be corrected
God is just too
God is wrathful
the Bible also says

It's just love.

And frankly, some of the most offensive passages in the Bible are all about love. I've learned that love, actually, is very offensive. Maybe the most offensive thing.

It's very offensive to say that God loves Hitler as much as Billy Graham. It's very offensive to say that the God loves ISIL as much as those who recently died in Orlando.

It's very offensive to say that love never fails and always trusts and is patient... and everything else in the list from 1 Corinthians because none of those words could be used to describe Hell.

And, for some unknown reason, it's very offensive to say that God will not torture people forever because that is, in no way, love.

It's very offensive to be told that we are just supposed to love.

And yet, it's one of the most freeing, simplifying, beautiful things on the planet.

Difficult? Yes. Inspiring? Yes. Evil? Not in any way.

Here are some verses that are in the actual Bible. If someone made these up and gave a sermon on them, they would be called the devil by many Christian groups.

If you do not love, you do not know God.

When Jesus talked about knowing God, he was talking to a bunch of people who said that they prayed, prophesied, performed miracles and all that good stuff. He says get out of here, you never knew me.

Saying a prayer is not knowing God.

Loving is.

Jesus also said that everyone loves their friends. That's not what we're talking about here.

A bigger, wider, all inclusive love.

If we love one another, God lives in us.

I assume there is where the idea of inviting God into our hearts came from. But the thing is, we don't invite God into our hearts with words. We love and God fills our being. Or, better, we love and become aware and acknowledge and start to know the God in us.

God is love. Whoever lives in love lives in God, and God in them.

A pretty amazing blend of the human and the divine seems to happen best, when we love.

There is no fear in love. But perfect love drives out fear, because fear has to do with punishment. The one who fears is not made perfect in love.

Hell is all about fear and punishment. Using Hell to convince anyone of God actually has nothing to do with God. In any way.

Going around the world being the fear and punishment police for society and individuals is not love.

Whoever does not love their brother and sister, whom they have seen, cannot love God, whom they have not seen.

Loving God is generally considered the thing. The end-all-be-all for many spiritual people. If you can not love ISIS, you can not love God. If you can not love homosexuals, you can not love God. If you can not love, Westboro Baptist, you can not love God. If you can not love evangelicals, you can not love God. If you can not love Donald Trump and Republicans, you can not love God. If you can not love Hillary Clinton and Democrats, you can not love God.

I think we get it. Plus, you know, I don't want to convict myself too much.

There are no groups, justified or not, we are not to love.

And, a reminder, love is patient, love always trusts, love keeps no record of wrongs.

Now, an important addition I've learned recently. Love does not mean we ignore our allergies.

I have a good friend who is allergic to sugar, brewer's yeast, and gluten. She can't have alcohol, candy, or bread. And she doesn't.

Some of us have allergies to certain people. They are bad for us. They damage our soul when we ingest them and, therefore, we are not to ingest them.

However, my good friend is thrilled when I enjoy a beer with her and her husband. She is happy that some people can eat handfuls of peanut M & M's while she can not. And she smiles at warm bread out of the oven and the smell of it.

She loves sugar, and hopes that people enjoy it for all it was meant to be. She, however, does not eat it.

He destroyed your heart. You can hope to love him and you can hope that someone can enjoy him for the man that he is, if he can find that self, but that does not mean you continue to date him.

She does nothing but heap shame on you. You're never a good enough parent, never a good enough boss, never a good enough wife. You can hope to love her, and you can hope that someone can enjoy her for the woman that she is, if she can find that true self, but that does not mean you continue to have morning coffee with her.

Allergies exist. They are real. They are toxic. They rob you of life and you have to create a life that avoids them while still hoping for love to win someday somehow.

And believing it already does with God.

So, love.

To love ourself is the most difficult thing to do on the planet.

To love others is easily the second most difficult.

And if you are able to do either of those even somewhat successfully, someone will hate you, and then loving that person will become very difficult.

043

love to argue vs argue to love.

I would imagine that humans have always enjoyed a good argument and I'm not one to say that we suddenly love it more. I do think we have more information than we ever have and so we have more ammunition to fire in our wars of words and opinions.

We also have more abilities to express our opinions without the fear of getting punched in the face because there is a technological wall between us and so... we probably argue a little more.

I grew up with three brothers who all have a wide spectrum of opinions on... everything. I always enjoy a good argument.

I do think we love to argue for one really good reason: it's hard to love when we are arguing and we really like any situation that is hard to love, because than we have excuses to not do it.

Too many people are really set on coming up with great reasons to not love someone, or at least not give there all to someone. Or, at least, not give a quarter to them if they are on the street.

We even find arguments on what love is so that we don't have to do it.

If we want to argue, can we argue about reasons to love someone rather than argue about reasons not to?

044

criticism and compliments.

My friend Jack told me a story of John Wesley apparently saying to his fellow-Christian and friend, George Whitefield, "Your God is my devil."

It's a clever little line. As I really thought about it, it started to blow my little mind.

Is it possible that someone would view the devil as God and/or view God as the devil?

Jesus told the Pharisees, who believed they were going to great lengths to convert people to God, that they were doing the complete opposite and, actually, converting people to Hell.

This would seem to imply that there are still a good many people who believe they are following the ultimate source of good in the universe who are actually following the ultimate sources of evil in the universe.

To be a little less dramatic, there are lots of people who believe they are feeding and living for something bigger than themselves, who are actually feeding and living for their own ego (which sometimes likes to act bigger than ourselves).

To put this all a different way, it would seem that what some people frame as a criticism, is actually a compliment. For instance, I was at an event where there were protesters and they were chanting that the person I was there to hear actually believes that

Hitler is in Heaven along with child pedophiles.

That only made me want to hear more from that person. I view that as a tremendous compliment. If someone said that about me, I would glow.

I've heard through the rumor mill/grape vine that our church doesn't talk about sin enough.

Interestingly enough, 1 John says that anyone born of God does not continue to sin. Jesus said to be perfect. Thomas Merton says the perfect have no need to reflect on the details of their actions.

Their criticism could actually be taken as a tremendous compliment.

There are many more examples.

(I suppose it's important to add my definition of "a critic" here: the point of a critic is only to point out faults to make themselves feel better.)

With all of this I've learned to take the critics with a grain of salt. Not because they are wrong, but simply because they are critics. Criticism is subjective. It's an opinion. It's often the opinion of someone who I find to be more devil than God… by nature of it being critical in the first place.

I've learned to be less critical. What if my God is my ego? What if my criticism is a compliment to them and will only encourage them in whatever they are doing so that I will only become more critical?

Be humble. Be complimentary. If the person wants to take it critically, that will be on them, and it will be of much more power anyway.

045

anything you can do i can do better.

My older brother used to taunt me with this line and it would drive me crazy. It still does. But I'll admit that I have used it on people who want to play the do it better game, which many religious people do.

If you want to call me a heretic, I can call you a heretic and do it better.

If you want to say I don't respect the Bible, I can say you don't respect the Bible, and do it better.

If you want to say I don't follow the true God, I can say you don't follow the true God and do it better.

If you want to say I don't believe in Jesus, I can say you don't believe in Jesus and do it better.

If you want to say I'm a wolf in sheep's clothing, I can say you are and do it better.

You see, it's just not a game that's good for anyone. What's the point, besides making the ego feel momentarily better?

It doesn't get us anywhere. So let's play a different game.

Where do you see God? Where do you experience God? How have you evolved in the last few years? How are you changing? What do you think needs to change? Why?

046

you.

I've had lots of words typed in this space. Sometimes you just let Richard Rohr talk, because when he does, he makes whatever you have typed or written sound stupid.

So...

In the spiritual life, there aren't too many absolutes I can make, but this is certainly one. On the spiritual journey, the message is always to you. The message s always telling you to change. Now, what most people do is they use religion to try to change other people. It's always someone else that needs changing. No. Stop it. Once and for all. Whatever happens to you in your life is a message to you. Oh the ego wants to avoid that. So we look for something out there to change–somebody not like me is always the problem.

047

the pain is real.

I have met a person who was told by her father that the world would be better off without her. Repeatedly. Over and over.

I have met a person who is dealing with cancer, again, and just watched two of her siblings die including a brother while choking on a piece of food after a successful surgery. She told me she is "broken".

I have met a person who lost her mom within 3 months of a diagnosis and is now getting ready to get married without her there to help her.

I have met a person who is one of only 80 people in the world with a certain genetic disorder.

I have a met a person who asked me if I did funerals because she believes her 21 year-old son will not be around much longer... he's had two overdoses this summer.

I have met a person whose father was recently diagnosed with ALS.

I have met a person who was repeatedly sexually abused by her step-father until the age of 12, lost her sister to suicide, and was addicted to pain-killers.

I have met a person whose parents told her to not bother coming home for Thanksgiving, because she was gay.

I have met a person who recently lost her husband to MS, after taking care of him for years. She still says "at some point I'm just going to start crying and not be able to stop".

I have met a person who was sexually and physically abused as a child.

I have met a person who was sexually and physically abused as a child by her parents who were on the elder board.

I have met a person whose wife took a nap one morning and never woke up because she took too many pills.

I have met someone who has tried to hang himself, shoot himself, and take an overdose, and said, I couldn't even kill myself the right way.

Writing these sentences, recalling these beautiful people, is causing me to cry as I type this at this very moment.

I haven't even mentioned miscarriages, addictions, teen moms, hundreds of illnesses, loneliness, eating disorders, broken relationships, doubt, frustration, or our 7 year-old neighbor who was hit by a car a couple of weeks ago and will never live anything close to a normal life again... and the list goes on and on.

The pain is real. It's hard. It's staggering. And there are no easy answers.

Sometimes it's just good to cry in it.

048

a certain beauty finds itself in the darkness.

Brené Brown wrote the above and her words were a theme for our season of Lent one year.

Every minute 300 million cells will die in our body.

Every 7 years we will have a new body.

In order for there to be something new, there must be space, In order for there to be space, something must die. It's happening constantly.

From Cynthia Borgeault: *For a seed to achieve its greatest expression, it must come completely undone. The shell cracks, its insides come out and everything changes. To someone who doesn't understand growth, it would look like complete destruction.*

I have met a person who was told by her father that the world would be better off without her. Repeatedly. Over and over.

And she is one of the strongest people I know.

I have met a person who is dealing with cancer, again, and just watched two of her siblings die including a brother while choking on a piece of food after a successful surgery. She told me she is "broken".

And yet, she is not.

I have met a person who lost her mom within 3 months and is now getting ready to get married without her.

We cried together after having met. She inspired me.

I have met a person who is one of only 80 people in the world with a certain genetic disorder.

She is one of the most brilliant, beautiful, and amazing humans on the planet. Changing lives.

I have a met a person who asked me if I did funerals because she believes her 21 year-old son will not be around much longer... he's had two overdoses this summer.

She said she won't stop loving her son. She hasn't.

I have met a person whose father was recently diagnosed with ALS.

He doesn't like to talk about, because there are lots of people with lots of problems.

I have met a person who was repeatedly sexually abused by her step-father until the age of 12, lost her sister to suicide, and was addicted to pain-killers.

She shared her story at our church and her strength was breath-taking and more moving than any sermon.

I have met a person whose parents told her to not bother coming home for Thanksgiving, because she was gay.

She has returned home.

I have met a person who recently lost her husband to MS, after taking care of him for years. She still says "at some point I'm just going to start crying and not be able to stop".

She is one of the most beautiful and strong people you will ever come across. At her daughter's wedding, recently, all the of the men in her daughter's life - brothers, brother-in-laws, father-in-law, friends, and, finally her daughter's new husband - danced with her on her first dance.

I have met a person who was sexually and physically abused as a child.

He has a wife and child of his own now. He smiles and laughs and feeds his son a bottle.

I have met a person who was sexually and physically abused as a child by her parents who were on the elder board.

She is finding a new god, who doesn't live in the land of fear.

I have met a person whose wife took a nap one morning and never woke up.

He wailed over her casket and said that she was an angel and he was a devil. I think he will learn that is not the case.

I have met someone who has tried to hang himself, shoot himself, and take an overdose, and said, I couldn't even kill myself the right way.

I told him it was an honor to meet him. I was moved in my soul to just shake his hand.

We are very afraid of the darkness, the pain, the suffering, and we do everything we can to avoid it... and yet, try as we may, we cannot deny it is built into the fabric of growth in our universe and there is something beautiful inside of it.

Indeed, the truth that many people never understand, until it is too late, is that the more you try to avoid suffering, the more you suffer, because smaller and more insignificant things begin to torture you, in proportion to your fear of being hurt.

The one who does most to avoid suffering is, in the end, the one who suffers the most: and his suffering comes to him from things so little and so trivial that one can say that it is no longer objective at all. It is his own existence, his own being, that is at once the subject and the= source of his pain, and his very existence and consciousness is his greatest torture… – Thomas Merton

Eat, drink, and be merry.

049

lent in any month.

Lent is the 40 days before Easter when human beings are supposed to spend some time in darkness. In doubt, frustrations, and raised fists. And uncertainty. It's a time when we don't have to know everything. That alone can be the most liberating feeling on the planet.

I've always been a person who leans into the dark side of life... a little. Depeche Mode was my band growing up. That foreboding, grungy feel just sat right with me and not because I was depressed but, looking back, because it felt more honest.

Lent is a chance to be honest.

One of the more powerful things I've ever been involved in at our church was a Lent service in which there were four black boards put in the middle of the room and all the chairs were removed.

We invited people to write their gripes, their complaints, their pain, their doubt, their anger on those walls in silver paint. We promised no answers, no solutions and no comfort... just the exhale of pain.

Reading those walls was stunning. To everyone.

Churches come off so clean and sparkly sometimes and this was nothing but dirty and messy honest reflections of sexual assault, addiction, anger at God (if God exists) and overall beautiful honesty of the hard things in life.

It's in the darkness where we learn that there is still good. It's in the darkness where we learn that life only comes from death.

It's in the darkness that we are honest and free to admit what life is actually like and to be okay with not knowing all the answers.

As I type this, yesterday we, again did something similar at our church. The microphone was added to those who wanted to express pain and uncertainty amidst the pain.

I found myself crying at the end of the service in front of the entire church - not something I usually do - but because it was so moving and powerful to be a part of.

I don't think it's the darkness we are afraid of. The fear of a cave is very different than the fear of the night sky. It might not be the dark but the lack of freedom we often perceive there to be within it.

I think we miss a lot by trying to disinfect our lives from anything close to darkness. When we do that we miss the chance to sit under the dark night sky and be overwhelmed by its majesty, mystery, and endless expansion and freedom.

I suppose giving up chocolate can be good, but spending time reflecting on and being honest about the pain, death, and suffering that surround us all the time, is even better.

Even in whatever month it is right now.

050

alleys.

No matter how great a city looks, you can always find an alley. The dark, lonely, dirty places that people are afraid of and where all the trash gets sent. The places where we are told not to walk and yet, where most of the work gets done. I always try to look down them.

People are like cities.
Businesses are like cities.
Churches are like cities.
Countries are like cities.
Systems are like cities.

Some call these “sacrifice zones” but no matter the term you want to use, there is a place where the hard parts of life must reside.

In the 1936 Olympic Games in Berlin, Hitler, and the rest of Germany, sought to hide their alleys. They wanted to put on a good presentation.

Jesus talked to religious leaders and told them they looked great on the outside but on the inside they were dead, much like 1936 Berlin.

I’m still afraid of alleys. I’m trying not to be. It seems like the only way we can change anything is to, first, acknowledge them and to, second, enter them.

051

too much fear.

It's everywhere, soaking everything and everyone in its ugly, toxic, noxious gas. It's probably the most prevalent thing I see in my own life and in the life of most everyone else. If we are those fish in that cave in Mexico, the poisonous plant is definitely fear.

People are afraid of church, afraid of God, afraid of Hell, afraid of standing out, afraid of not standing out, afraid of old ideas and new ideas, afraid of bad theology, or any theology, afraid of large groups of people they have never met, afraid of people they have met who are not like themselves, afraid of failure and thus risk, afraid of not being enough, of not doing enough, of not measuring up, afraid of not knowing enough, or knowing the right things, afraid of new paths, new direction, new thoughts, new people, new wine-skins, and afraid of not being afraid. We are afraid of freedom, mystery, and of wide open expanses of awe and wonder.

It all reminds me of my favorite Pixar short "Day and Night" which quotes Wayne Dyer and maybe, during this time in our country, should be read daily.

Fear of the unknown.
They are afraid of new ideas.

They are loaded with prejudices, not based upon anything in reality, but based on... if something is new, I reject it immediately because it's frightening to me. What they do instead is just stay with the familiar.

You know, to me, the most beautiful things in all the universe, are the most mysterious.

We're actually afraid of change, which to go back to those fish, is the only way we can survive.

Is there anything more evil than that?

There is a great little parable, from Anthony DeMello, we had on our church wall for a while. It should be on everyone's wall.

What is love?

The absence of fear.

What is it that people fear?

Love.

We're even afraid of not being afraid. How messed up is that? Maybe even more evil than being afraid to change to survive and not be afraid...

Sometimes I think this whole spiritual life is only about one thing: stop being afraid. Jesus repeated this pretty often. As did angels.

As did God.

Elizabeth Gilbert, among many, talk about putting fear in its place. Not being afraid doesn't mean we never have fear, it just means we know what to do with it and we don't let it drag us around the world by its leash.

And we do that by not being afraid of real, unconditional, love. And knowing we're enough and worthy and loved.

052

hate your father and mother?

That statement from Jesus has always been really frustrating to me. Even the explanations which always involved original languages, and lots of "well..." never did it.

One day I was with a girl who was raised in a very conservative family. She was starting to question much of what she had been raised with. She was finding some freedom, getting the sense that she could unload quite a bit of religious baggage and start running in the fields.

But her parents. Man, they kept warning her and telling her she was bordering on heresy and bringing all of their own fears into their life.

And as the conversation went on, they were holding this poor girl back. They were keeping her in the cage.

And I said, you know there is that verse... which was the first time I'd ever used that verse in a way that didn't annoy me.

Hate in the Hebrew world implied separation.
Love implied clinging or moving toward.

Hate fear. Always. Sometimes, parents are the greatest fear-mongers on the planet. If they are. When they are. Move away from that part of them and move toward God.

053

freedom can bring fear.

I watched a video of some lab monkeys being freed. They had been stuck in cages for years, experimented on by people in white coats.

They were living an absolutely terrible life.

They released the monkeys. They opened up the cages and allowed them to feel sunlight, to run into trees, to race across a field of grass.

Some of them bolted. They were so pumped and stoked that they could hardly believe it. They were laughing in the top branches of the nearby trees.

Others sat in the sun like we sit in the sun in March after not seeing it for 3 months. You just can't believe something that fills up so much of our space, that costs nothing, feels that good. These monkeys were in heaven.

But some... well they just sat by the door. What is this? Sunlight? Grass? Trees? I think I prefer the beautiful four white walls and the man who gives me my food every day and pokes me with needles.

I assume you see where this is going but in case you don't.

Religion has been an experiment on a lot of people. It has poked and prodded and kept people very very under control in a nice tight box. People grew to love that box. And when someone comes along and starts talking about life, and God and love, well some people literally start crying while sitting in that sunlight. They can't believe it.

But others, say no thank you and head back to the cage. Maybe it's too much space. Too many things could go wrong. Too many risks. Too many what if's. The cage hurts but at least it's safe.

God led people out of the cages of slavery and production in Egypt and the first thing they wanted to do was go back. God always leads people out of cages and will perform plagues just to prove how serious God is about getting out of cages.

Safety, unfortunately, often wins. There is a fear in freedom and love and not being forced to make bricks for a Pharaoh that beats you up.

The problem is that God is not safe. Life is not safe. Love is not safe. Love demands freedom. It struggles to be noticed in that cage.

I used to get really angry at people who go back in the cage but I have learned that God is in the cage too. God is in there, trying with everything God can do, to lead people out into the field, or wilderness, or life beyond where they can be big and God can be big while still finding room for both of them to breathe.

At least, I hope, because I'm sure I still have cages and blind spots I don't quite see and I trust there is more freedom.

I just keep trying to point out there... to move out there... toward the sunlight where love embraces all and there is not the fear we think there is.

054

independence.

Jesus should feel like the cage being blown to pieces.

Jesus frees us from purity codes, from ritual, from religion, from doctrine, from theories, from head-games, from guilt, from blindness, to help us see a beautiful, inspiring, bold, revolutionary, optimistic, abundant, generous new world.

To see love.

Pharisees still hate Jesus. They prefer captivity and fear and control and power.

As long as they are on top.

Get free.

055

people love to be beat.

Yeah, that sounds really bad but I heard it from a retired Nazarene pastor who, obviously meant it figuratively, and I, very sadly, agree with him.

He said, "People like being beat and they don't know what to do when they aren't."

It's really hard for people to be told they don't have to bring anything to the altar to offer to their god.

How else are we supposed to know where we stand?

Humans are much better off in a church/job/relationship/God that doesn't beat them. People don't need to feel terrible about themselves, to wallow in misery, in order to feel good about themselves. And yet, I'm always surprised with how many people still live in that place.

It speaks volumes of what religion has done to the divine human spirit. It's tragic on universal proportions.

I've got to feel worse... to feel better. That is the lie that must die.

Today.

056

if the bible is...

There are times when the Bible has not been awesome to me. At all.

When the Bible is God's authoritative word, or without error, or the handbook to life, or a science book, or anything else along those lines, I find it to be a terrible book. When people use it that way, I find myself really trying hard to be quiet.

However.

If the Bible is a book written by humans in a cultural context of language, understanding, and perspective…

If the Bible is more like a menu…

If the Bible is the world's greatest myth...

If the Bible is a compost pile... providing material for new...

If the Bible is story, because story is what still speaks to us after thousands of years whether it actually occurred or not…

If the Bible is supposed to inspire us to live our own stories of God and not to just memorize other peoples' stories…

Then I find it to be a rather inspiring, creative, eye-opening record of the evolution of humanity, of God, of myself, and of the world…

057

good villains and bad heroes.

The Bible is filled with apparent heroes. Heroes of the faith. I use the word very loosely, because, the more I've spent looking and hearing about these people, I'm not sure any of them measure up to Batman.

We did a series on 1 Samuel and one of my big take-aways was this: Samuel was a jerk. He put Saul in one of the worst positions possible. He put an inordinate amount of pressure on Saul to be this amazing king and then threw him under the bus whenever he could.

This guy was not a hero and we named the book after him?

Then comes David. Oh great King David. If you play out his little war deception and murdering of villages so his deception wouldn't get out to other countries... if you translate that story in modern times with US military and ISIS as the characters, well, we would hate David. He's a selfish traitor. That's before he kills a guy under his control so he can take his wife.

Solomon was called out by God for doing the same thing that Egypt had done. Building a military superpower on the backs of slave labor and trusting in chariots. He was the wise King?

And even Joseph. The great Joseph - one of the greatest stories in all the Bible. Pretty amazing to think that the reason that Jews were enslaved in Israel was because of Joseph.

He stocked up a bunch of Pharaoh's crops during a famine and then charged the Israelites (his own people) for seven consecutive years, eventually demanding their enslavement as payment.

And we could go on and on but what's the point?

There are no good guys and bad guys. Pharisees wanted to put labels on good guys and bad guys. They loved pointing out the bad guys thinking they were the good guys.

Unfortunately, they ended up killing the good guy and becoming the bad guys themselves.

We spend a lot of time calling out bad guys. Maybe the good guys recognize that the bad guys are just like them and maybe the bad guys still think there are good guys and bad guys.

058

my movie idea.

Imagine Red Dawn. Or any other action/war movie that you've seen.

The premise is that China has set-up military bases on U.S. soil and started to come down on religious rules and laws. You know the kind of stuff that really gets people in this country riled up. They have called us barbaric and ridiculed our faith and banned our guns.

The entire movie is this group of rogue soldiers who are camping out in the mountains and fighting the Chinese, standing up for American freedom, and kicking some butt.

The whole time they are also planning out something - something big. Something that will put the Chinese on their heels. We get tidbits of it but never what it is until the last scene.

Downtown Beijing.
Early morning.
Skyscrapers everywhere.
Two planes fly into them.

Roll credits.

Good guys and bad guys gets real confusing, depending on perspective.

059

culture and science help us read the bible.

Talk about a line that will scare the soul out of some people.

We're all trying to figure this stuff out. We all always have been.

And the Bible is a story of people trying to do that. And so is science. And so is culture.

And so, as science discovers that the Earth is 13.8 billion years old, that evolution is a thing, that quantum mechanics is real, that dark matter and dark energy are also real, we get to discover new ways to read this book about humans trying to figure out how to discover God. In all of those things.

And so, as society discovers that women are actually just as valuable as men, that human beings should never own other human beings, that the Earth is valuable, that there is room for all of us, we discover new ways to read this book about humans trying to figure out how to discover God. In all of those things.

There's no need to continue this fight with culture and science. Instead lets embrace it, learn from it, and be a part of its expansion.

090

our brains and the bible, like that, don't work.

Study of the human brain is one of the most amazing, frustrating, enchanting, and fear-inducing topics ever.

But it's downright enlightening when it comes to religion and the Holy Books.

Let's start here:

We are figuring out all kinds of things about the brain including memory. Autobiographical episodic memory is one of the ways we store information and autobiographical episodic memory is pieced together from experiential moments that we retrieve. Those moments are affected by our knowledge, our mood, the social context, our physical perspective, and even language. So we encode these memories based on all of those things and retrieve them based on those things.

Thus, every time we retrieve a memory, psychologists say it's contaminated, and, of course, affected by the list above.

So when we say we remember something. Yes, we do. But probably not what actually happened.

Then throw in all of these ingredients:

Confirmation bias. We all do it. We get a belief, lock it in place and then screen everything through that belief. We hear and see in a biased way in order to confirm the thing we already believe. In other words, two people could read the same article and come away with the idea that the article is proving their own belief.

This happens in many experiments. The same article will make one person feel more correct in their assumption of global warming being false and another person will feel more correct in their assumption that it is true.

The same words, perceived differently.

Optimism bias: This is another thing we all have, sometimes called better-than-average effect. This is the way we look at ourselves as better than everyone else. Or in a more positive light.

This also works when we are talking about our own risks. We think very differently about the risk of someone walking "downtown at night" than we do about ourselves walking "downtown at night". The risk is usually lower for ourselves than for the general population.

Hindsight bias: We always make the past appear better than it was. In large part, because we now know, looking back, that all those fears we had about the past, didn't pan out. So, looking back, it feels safer, less frightening and overall better than the time we are in... where we don't know how those fears are going to pan out.

A great example from the book The Science of Fear (which everyone should read) was an article by Thomas Friedman in 2003 about how great 1985 was.

However, in 1985 the Cold War was raging, AIDS was ready to be an epidemic and there were a whole host of other fears... that all turned out alright. So we go back and remember 1985 as being much better than it was.

One more: Whenever our brains move a "mystical" experience from the part of our brain that stores "experiences that we can't put into words" into the section of our head that is language and

words… we, of course, alter the actual experience. In fact, those two section of the brain don't really work together.
So when we try to explain the sunset, just by trying to explain it, we alter it in our own brain, before saying a word.

Now if you stir all of that into a bowl, what do you end up?

A group of people having mystical experiences and then trying to confirm their bias about being chosen by God in a certain context, knowledge, perspective and culture and then writing stories about those experiences while trying to retrieve those memories and looking back thinking things were much better than they actually were and thinking they were better than most people around them as well.

People collect these stories, letters, and ideas and then read them with their own bias, perspective, mystical experiences, etc…

And then have the audacity to say that they are infallible, inherent, and other fancy words that ignore just about everything about humanity, brains, and how we experience life.

The Rabbis said there were 77 interpretations to every passage of Scripture and only 1 right interpretation that no one but God knows.

Thank God for the Rabbis.

061

maslow.

Maslow's hierarchy of needs is a theory of psychology written in 1943, which focuses on the stages of growth in humans.

The stages go something like this:

physiological: air and water
safety: personal security, health and well-being
love/belonging: friendship, intimacy, and family
esteem: a sense of contribution or value
self-actualization: the realization of potential.

They are great. Stealing from the great Joseph Campbell I learned something though. And gave it my own interpretation.

Pursuing those things is not where life is found. Campbell talks about myths and the value of myths. Myths bring awe and wonder back into the world and provide a bigger and more mysterious story to live into. That is their power.

Toward the end of his life Maslow even added another level: self-transcendence. "The self only finds it actualization in giving itself to some higher goal outside oneself, in altruism or spirituality."

And someone who is not living into myth, well, they are not living life to the fullest.

We all know that someone who must walk for 8 hours a day for basic water is surviving but not living.

The same could be said for someone who must work 8 hours a day to realize their own potential. They are surviving but not living.

That is why the myth, if you want to call it that, that a divine power that contains and is expanding the universe to ever greater and brighter and more beautiful arenas, and that lives within me and you and is pulling me somewhere I can not imagine, if I just let go of all the pursuits and realize I'm enough in this moment, right now, is where life actually might start to begin.

If we go one step further, every good myth contains some main parts - the hero's journey as Campbell called it.

The Summons, the Wilderness, the Gift, and the Return.

So, this divine power containing and expanding and letting us know we are enough and bringing us to better life is not all magic fairies.

It's bravery to go new places with our thoughts, it's the courage to be in the places of pain and suffering, it's the gift of realizing we're okay, even there, and it's returning with something majestic and motivating for those who are still are where we once were.

I agree with Campbell - we need better myths and better explanation of the myths of the Bible and those we are living.

062

church and dating.

I planted a church. The first Sunday was very similar to a first date. I had high hopes and expectations and so did the other people but none of us knew if it would work. It was a little awkward but also exciting.

As the years went by, we started to realize we liked each other and things got comfortable and beautiful. And the relationship is working.

About 9 months ago, we had our 5 year anniversary party that was a lot like a wedding reception with dancing, drinking, music and toasts. I think we're all married now.

This has all made me think of all the other commonalities between churches and dating, some of which might help you in either... or both.

There are good churches and good people and sometimes the two aren't a good fit. It doesn't mean anything bad about them, or you.

There are bad churches. Really bad ones. Abusive churches. Friends don't let friends date them or stay committed to them.

There are churches that really sell you on the first date and go all out. Then they end up not really caring too much after you have committed.

Breaking up is hard. Even if the relationship was bad. You still carry some grief. If it was good, you carry even more. Acknowledge it when and if you move on.

Relationships take time to build. You can't replicate in 3 weeks what took 3 years to build, unless it's magic. (But don't always expect magic.)

Beauty is in the eye of the beholder. Don't knock a church because her hair is too long or she wears too much make up. Someone might love her. Don't love a church because she's the cheerleader and everyone at school says she's the hottest one of the bunch.

Love a church because she's beautiful. To you.

063

the church is beautiful.

I understand very well that the church has absolutely destroyed some people out there. (Well people acting in the name of "the church" but let's not get hung up on details...)

I get it. I'm floored by some of the stories of people who still go to church after what the church has done to them. I tell them frequently: I can't believe you're here. I honestly can't.

But here's the thing. Many of us have also been absolutely destroyed by a boyfriend, girlfriend, partner, wife, husband, boss, co-worker, stranger, cashier, friend... you get the idea. By a human being.

And we still believe there are some good humans and we seek them. (If we're in a good place, we still believe the person that hurt us is a good person and there are reasons they hurt us that we hope we can better understand, they can better understand, and we can all heal.)

I encourage you to keep looking. There are some beautiful, astounding, majestic, generous, inspiring, creative, thoughtful, human beings who make the churches they attend much the same.

064

more church and dating.

When I had my first daughter I was petrified. I was scared of the horrible guys that would come and try to date her and want one thing from her and how bad it would be to have to fend them off with shotguns.

I shared this at a church in my first year of pastoring.

A lady came up to me after the sermon and said, Ryan, you're all wrong. Why are you dreading your daughters dating so much? We have three daughters and the men they have brought into our family have been the best thing to ever happen to us. Why don't you start thinking of it that way?

I never forgot her words. (I later told her that they changed my life.)

In fact, I took them further. Why was it that I told my daughters that men were pigs and wanted nothing from them but to get down their pants? Wouldn't that mean if my daughters started dating a guy who was a pig wanting nothing but to get down her pants that she would think... well that's what dad always told me guys were?

So, I started talking differently to my daughters(s) and changing my head in the process. I can't wait for my daughters to start dating. Guys are amazing. Guys are awesome. I can't wait to see who they fall head over heels for.

I can't wait to see the amazing human being that they bring home.

And all of this is like church.

Have you noticed all that articles, blog posts, and comments about how bad the church is lately? When people go to a church and it sucks, doesn't everyone think, well… I guess this is what everyone said. Churches suck. If I want to go to any church, it's going to suck so I might as well not go to any or go to one that sucks.

Self-fulfilling prophecy, I believe, it's called.

What about if we started talking about how awesome church is? How fulfilling. How well it spends it's money. How relevant and inspiring and graceful and loving it is?

065

church is friends.

I'm not in this to fight for anyone's business like a fast food restaurant, an airline, or a cell phone provider. I'm in this to free and inspire people and to point toward something refreshing for the exhausting game of life we're all playing. If the language and culture we speak and work in, helps to do that, great. If not, well, I understand.

That said, I get sad when people leave. Not because it's somehow a bad reflection of our church or how we do things, but, quite simply, because I won't see them anymore. And that stinks. As much as we hate to admit it, I stay connected with a large amount of people through church. And when they leave, I will miss them. So will others.

So don't mistake the sadness for business. We miss people. We miss relationships. And, again, that's why we say, if we do run into you in the store, please don't ignore me and act embarrassed.

We're still humans, right?

990

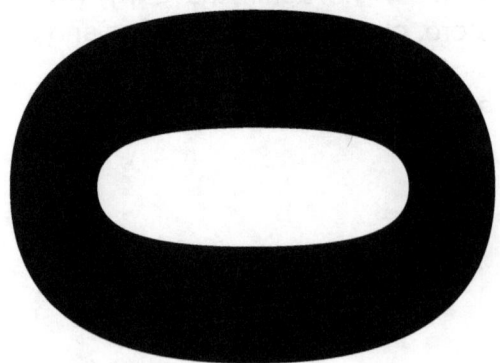

fire and gasoline.

If you ever watch a fighter jet take off, you'll notice a tremendous amount of fire coming out the rear of the airplane. If you think about fire, you'll remember that fire and gasoline, when combined in the wrong ways, will kill you and everyone close to the combination.

And yet, when you see this jet, with a huge flame sticking out its back, being fueled by gasoline, we remember, fire and gasoline if separated enough, fuel one of the most powerful hair-raising sights on the planet.

Church and money. Wow, I tremble just typing the two words together.

We have to figure out how to keep the fire away from the gasoline in order that the gasoline can fuel the fire that makes the jet fly.

Churches are still trying to figure that out.

Some things our own church has tried to do to keep them separate that sometimes work and sometimes don't.

We don't pass plates. We never have. It's amazing how many pastors and "church leaders" have told me that we need to pass plates because we "would make more money" and because "it puts pressure on people".

We have emptied our bank account three consecutive years and given it away.

We don't keep a savings account.

We give money to whomever asks with a need. If we have it, we give it. Period.

Money is awesome when we use it to fuel the forward movement. We will continue to try and figure out how to do it.

And if you have ideas as to how, please, please, please speak loudly!

067

church and community thoughts.

Church and community are two words that often feel like they are in a bad marriage. They are stuck together and don't really like each other. I mean they had a good run but things just aren't really working anymore.

And it's not for a lack of trying. There are small groups, community groups, luncheons, breakfasts, retreats, classes, service opportunities, studies, clubs, and functions all throughout the week. There are dedicated "meet someone new times" there are greeters and ushers and all kinds of other people who are supposed to make this community thing happen.

Of course, because the marriage is supposed to be great, churches will usually act like it is. Everyone here is best friends. We eat together, pray together, walk the neighborhood together, and, sometimes, even sleep together. We do life together. Want to join into our amazing circle of friends?

If your church is not filled with vibrant community, pastors should lead better, read more books, go to more community conferences, or really challenge the community to start acting more like a community.

I used to take a lot of the community or lack of community personally as though I had to do more.

I don't know anymore.

Here's what I've learned.

1. Some people do want community and they can't get it. These people break my heart. They break it because I want to give them a friend but I can't. Friends take time and they take two parties. One person wanting a friend can not simply be given a friend. They have to find someone who wants to be a friend.

I equate community to coral. Coral will grow just about anywhere except in empty flowing ocean water. However, put an old ship in the water and, over time, it will start to grow.

Every church has at least a piece of wire in the ocean. Coral will eventually attach. But there is absolutely nothing the church can do to force coral to attach. Some will build really big shipwrecks, and pump all kinds of nutrients that help coral, but in the end, it still has to grow on its own.

2. Some people don't think they want community.

Many people are simply afraid. To make friends you have to vulnerable and risk. Some people don't want to be vulnerable and/or risk and often for very good reasons. The church's job is to encourage vulnerability and risk and to be there when it hurts.

And then let coral grow.

3. Some people have community and are doing it outside the church.

Churches love to label everything with their brand. It's our small group, our Sunday morning, our Bible study. The thing is that many people have all kinds of community in all kinds of places that are not labeled City Church A. We should encourage that and let it be.

4. Some people need to not talk to a person.

There are many people who shouldn't talk to one person on a Sunday morning. They are exhausted. They are tired. They need to rest and breathe and relax and remember they are enough and worthy and loved and life still exists and beats all around them. There are many people like this and they are often berated at churches for not building community. Churches need to be berated for putting more burdens on them than they already carry.

Someone once called our church, church for adults. If you want something you have to go get it. I found this to be an incredible compliment for all the reasons listed above.

I don't know where everyone is at on every given Sunday.

I do know that many people who complain that they can't find community at a church will never find a church that gives them community. They'll go on lots of first dates - because first dates always seem hopeful - but they won't find a lasting relationship with a church until they stop complaining about life not being what they want and start trying to be a different person.

I do know that some people who don't need another friend, need to be a friend to someone who does. This is hard and this is sacrifice and it costs. This is not for everyone but it is for some people. They have to figure out if that's them.

I do know relationships (and coral) take time. You can't leave a church of 10 years and say you haven't found friends like you had at your old church after being at the new church for 6 months.

I do know people who come into a community with the ability to be slightly vulnerable and to take some risks, embed into that community much faster than people who wait for someone to approach them and offer them a friend.

I do know that many people who complain that they've never been invited to ______'s house, have never invited ______ to their house.

I do know that life is complicated and busy and full and that whenever I take a moment to connect in a meaningful way to another human being, I'm living more than I was with whatever complicated, busy and full thing I was doing previously.

890

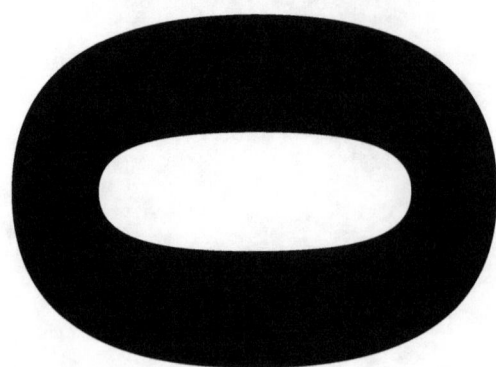

this really needs to be done now.

Women can do anything men can do. (I know, I know, we are biologically different. Stop with the excuses.)

They can preach, teach, lead, elder, deacon, whatever other "leadership" or "power" or "control" label you want to put on the task. They are leaders. They deserve power and control no matter what men think.

In fact, they can do many of those things better than men.

In fact, they should also be paid and treated the same as men who do the same job.

In fact, we are missing out on huge swaths of wisdom and inspiration because we don't push them to the front as often.

In fact, God has feminine qualities. The Bible speaks of them all the time including in the very beginning when humans (that's man and woman) were created in God's image. The two form God's image.

In fact, when we ignore those qualities, it's easy to focus on intellectual and institutional functions and aspects of the church and ignore the more mystical.

In fact, still not knowing what to do with women, may be hurting the church more than anything else.

690

she.

These words need to be repeated more often than they are.

God is as much woman as God is man.

The feminine is as powerful as the male.

The feminine is as strong as the male.

The feminine is as full of wisdom as the male.

The feminine is as capable as the male.

The feminine is as deserving as the male.

The feminine is as important as the male in the life of the male and the female.

The feminine voice needs to be louder, only because it's still making up for lost time and lost resources.

070

if you can't praise them what are you?

Steph Curry tore up the NBA this season. A few nights after he set the record for 3 pointers and won the game on a ridiculous almost half-court shot. Average Joe's (not fans) were watching the replays on their iPhones and getting huge grins on their faces.

In the middle of the Steph Curry show - which it was - there were quite a few ex-NBA players saying things like...

Never seen anything like SCurry? Remind you of Chris Jackson /Mahamoud Abdul-Rauf, who had a short brilliant run in NBA?

Phil Jackson said that. Phil Jackson who has coached more championship teams than any other coach. What?

Oscar Robinson, an NBA legend, Charles Barkley and Walt Frazier all made comments that the game of basketball had changed and Curry, basically, isn't as great as everyone thinks.

Compare that to Lebron James who tweeted...

Never before seen someone like him in the history of ball!

And Baron Davis, Rudy Gay, Dwayne Wade who all couldn't stop gushing about his skills.

(It's interesting that LeBron James went on to beat Curry in the finals.)

This, of course, is not just a basketball thing. But it seems like there are two reactions to someone's success: jealousy and/or negative reactions to the new operating system or simple enjoyment of the evolution of "the game" and the fact that someone is doing what they were made to do and you get to be there for it and learn from it.

If I'm honest, sometimes it's hard not to be jealous. I spend all this time working on my craft, trying to get better, and here they come...

They're so lucky.
They aren't even that good.
It must be easy for them.
If they had to play the way I had to play.

Just the ego responding to fear.

So, I ask myself some questions...

If I can't look at another artists' work and say it is good, what kind of an artist am I?

If I can't read another author and say that is amazing, what kind of an author am I?

If I can't listen to another speaker and say wow, what kind of speaker am I?

If I can't listen to another musician and be overwhelmed, what kind of musician am I?

If I can't see another person dance and cheer for them, what kind of dancer am I?

If I can't appreciate the people who are honing their craft with more skill and talent than I am, if I can't be inspired by them, well... critics are everywhere. And they are terrified of their own standings.

Critics are never the actual artists, authors, speakers, musicians, and dancers because they are too busy taking down the people that are, while believing they could do it better than all of them. Or, at the least, making excuses for their success compared their own.

If I can't appreciate a different religion or faith perspective...

071

the bell man.

Speaking of jealousy... let's call it the Rob Bell phenomenon. I use Rob because a) he's been incredibly influential to me and b) he's such a great illustration of how threatened we become with change.

Some thoughts.

1. Rob Bell is the single biggest influence of my faith. Poets, Prophets, and Preachers in 2009 changed my life. I had been a pastor for a year at that time and I came back from the event and realizing I had converted to something. I was suddenly overwhelmed at the beauty of trees, overwhelmed that there was good in this world and overwhelmed that my pessimism was fading and becoming replaced by something good and optimistic. The good news was actually getting good and Rob Bell was a conduit of that good news.

2. People hate Rob Bell. Many use those exact words. People picket. Friends of mine jab at "Christian Celebrity". Other friends constantly make remarks about where Rob is going or "nervousness".

3. C.S. Lewis wrote: *Hatred has its pleasures it is therefore often the compensation by which a jealous man reimburses himself for the miseries of fear.*

People hate/dislike Rob Bell because they are jealous. And afraid. Afraid he might be more popular than them, afraid he might be right, afraid he might sway people away from their own belief which might mean that his belief is more appealing? I don't know. When you hate, you fear. Whenever you hate or meet someone who hates, ask yourself - or him or her - what you are afraid of.

4. I'm not saying Rob Bell is Jesus. I am saying the way that people respond to him is exactly how people responded to Jesus. Jealousy over the crowds. Anger at the way he uses the scriptures. And fear how he blows up the religious system. Right. Those same Pharisees still hate people who blow up the system and yet, if the system doesn't evolve, it dies.

Ironic. The same system the Pharisees are trying to save will definitely die if they succeed in saving it. (Probably why Jesus was always trying to warn them.)

5. Rob Bell steals from everyone. When you start reading the books that he reads, you realize he's just stealing stuff from everyone else. Which is awesome. He's not coming up with this stuff alone and you can steal from them too. And there's something that has been moving in this faith for a long time... that's always comforting. This faith has always had narrow roads of growth and life.

6. Rob Bell is not my friend. I really wanted him to be and really tried to make him my friend. He's not. That's cool. I'm finally okay with it. My wife told him how much he has meant to us. I told him the same. That's all that matters.

7. Rob Bell just speaks my language. We all have a language we speak and I'm not saying Rob Bell speaks the best or correct language but he does he speak mine. If Rob Bell isn't the person that speaks your language, please find people that do.

At the end of the day this has nothing to do with Rob Bell. This has to do with people who best help you to see who you are and what you are capable of.

Find him/her/them!

072

pausing.

Can I pitch counselors for a second?

Counselors are good for everyone. Everyone. People who are in tough spots and people who are in good spots. Everyone can improve. I've seen a variety of them and I'm seeing one now.

Counselors have permission to say it like it is. No one else on this planet does. You think they do, but they don't. Or the person you are talking to thinks they don't.

Counselors get paid to just listen to you and you don't have to feel guilty for not "asking them how they are doing"... Right? Isn't that fantastic? You can simply share your story, your views, and they just listen and talk, if you need them to.

Counselors know what to say. When they do talk, they are able to get right to it because they don't have to worry about permission and beating around the bush. You're there to hear it and they get to just say it. And they've been trained in what to say. Bonus!

I often wonder if we called counseling a different name, maybe it would blow up like hot yoga, CrossFit, and mindfulness. Maybe if we kept pitching it as something that keeps you evolving, instead of a mental prescription for a unhealthy mind and spirit, more people would be less afraid of it and likely to start it.

Have you heard of Pausing?

It's becoming very popular in LA and New York, and I think it's really finding some traction. The tradition comes from the East, where it has been practiced for years. Pausing is about finding someone "who listens and talks softly" to encourage humans to stop and think about important things in life with someone of care. People all over are the world are starting to pause and claiming it's working wonders.

You should try it.

Some places even practice a form of it on Sunday mornings, I hear.

073

sex.

As a pastor, I am often asked about sex. Ignoring the fact, I find that very strange - very rarely do people ask me to be on a panel about capitalism - it's a reality of the job that I've come to accept. (Actually, I don't know that I've ever even heard of a panel about capitalism.)

So, admittedly, when the sex topic comes up, I have to check myself from becoming critical or arrogant. It is a thing and I do understand that. It is a powerful thing and I do understand that. I happen to agree with Jessica Valenti that the thing has been made into way too much of a thing by the church, but again, it's a thing so it is worth talking about.

Rob Bell, James Cordan and Russel Brand will be the featured speakers in my sex talk summary.

Rob Bell wrote that "Sex is not the search for something that's missing. It's the expression of something that's been found."

James Cordan wrote in Glamour Magazine that "Everything is always about sex but sex is always about something else."

Russel Brand wrote "We have been told that freedom is the ability to pursue our petty, trivial desires when true freedom is freedom from these petty, trivial desires."

And boom.

That's it.

It's never about sex, or pornography, or affairs. Sex is oil on the surface of the water when there is something else happening on the bottom of the ocean a thousand feet away. We see the oil so we try to spend time cleaning it up but there are bigger problems.

There are no rules as to when to have sex and when not to. That's just cleaning up surface oil.

Married people have destructive sex.
Unmarried people have redemptive sex.

It's always the something else.

Brené Brown even makes the point that pornography is more often about shame than anything else. There is no fear of vulnerability and rejection when looking at pornography - and so it's appealing.

Now that's root of the problem stuff. The something else. The freedom.

Of course all of this takes time and self-analysis and puts the responsibly on us, so sometimes it's easier to put together a nice and tidy rule we can or can not follow... and those can be helpful if you don't want to spend the time thinking. But search for the "something else" and you'll know what to do with the sexuality - and how to be truly free.

074

marriage is...

...fading. Most of the statistics seem to point to less and less people getting married, which is a big worry for some. And that make sense.

...The most amazing relationship that two people can have together, in my opinion. I absolutely love being married. Which is why I'm all for more people getting married. Gay, straight or anything else. If there is fidelity, freedom, commitment and love... well I'm all for more of it.

... not the end-all-be-all to make everything-good-with-us-and-God. It's a consolation. It's better than not having any marriage in a society, especially a society where women were treated like property so God came up with marriage. Hey, this will make things better. Perfect? No. Better? Hopefully. Is it still? I think?

... never really modeled all that well, throughout the entire Bible, if you really think about it. Can anyone show me one example of a married couple in the entire Bible that would fit the description of a "good married couple" in today's Christian society?

... really really cultural. Someone was recently telling me that they think the United States is going to start having more polygamy. I don't know if I agree but I do know that one of the wisest people to ever live according to the Bible had hundreds of wives. (Man, that Bible gets tricky when you want it to be a guide book for human life.)

... not the most important thing in life. If I'm honest, 90% of the most influential, inspiring, motivating, wise, people in my life were not or are not married. Okay, I don't know if 90% is accurate but a lot of what has shaped me in my walk with God and life was thought of by someone who wasn't married. Jesus included.

... changing. That's alright. It, like most things, has already changed quite a bit and will probably continue to.

075

real grace and mercy.

100% grace and mercy...
without any qualifiers...
is...

...Hell to the ego.
...Heaven to the Divine.

076

lgbtq.

You are valuable, you are worthy, you are beautiful, you are powerful. You are love. There is nothing more that needs to be done or can be done to make the authentic you any more of those things.

Believe it. Accept it. Have faith in it.

I do realize the church has not made it easy to believe, accept or have faith. For that, I hope you reject the church that has done that to you and not the light that shines inside of you, right now, just as you are.

077

not working.

There is a huge difference in quitting because something is work and in quitting because something is not working.

There is a huge difference in not quitting when something is work and in not quitting when something is not working.

There are costs to both, but they are not the same costs. One will give you life and one will kill you. Sometimes literally.

Some of the most inspiring stories are stories of people who work tremendously hard to make something happen. To make that dream come true. To write. To speak. To teach. To travel. To be a comedian. To get on stage. To travel to Mars. Their stories are always the same... filled with work.

The other half of the most inspiring stories are stories of people who quit because they recognize they are prolonging someone else's dream and putting effort and hours into something that simply doesn't work. A teacher who quit to tend bar. A lawyer who quit to open a Yoga studio. An engineer who became a nudist. A neurologist who quit and opened a restaurant. Their stories are always the same... ending work.

There is a massive difference in being afraid of work and being afraid of work that doesn't work.

There are many voices, many who will benefit greatly from us working on a job that doesn't work, who will tell us to keep working. Make sure it's working.

078

bricks.

Let's get back to Pharaoh for a second.

Imagine a little scenario, if you will.

You are living in Egypt as a Hebrew slave. You go to work every day to make bricks. Good-bye honey, off to make some bricks. Love you.

Day after day.

But, of course, some things change.

Honey! I quit making bricks for those idiots. I'm now making bricks at a better spot. You should see these bricks. I mean they are so much nicer. And we cut them a little bit differently. It's a much smoother cut. I think these bricks are going to be used on the new pyramid we are building! The really nice one!

Oh, honey, I'm so proud of you. Do they beat you there?

Oh, yeah, of course. But much less! Most people only get a few lashings!

Day after day.

But, of course, some things change.

Honey, tough day at work. Things aren't going well. They've raised the quotas. I'm going to be staying later. More work to do.

These new bricks are really in high demand and Pharaoh wants more of them. He's also informed everyone that he's found us lazy. Apparently, he's not been happy. It means later nights.

I'm so sorry, honey. But, hey, at least we have meat and stew to eat for dinner!

I know! You're right! It's so true. I mean what's our other option? Go wander around a desert and eat dew off the ground? Can you imagine how much we would miss our stew? It's definitely worth it. Besides, this is legacy stuff. These pyramids will be around forever... and I was a part of it.

Day after day.

Now, thank goodness, none of us live this story today. No one would be so stupid as to trap themselves into certainty and pay-checks and abuse in order to earn a living and pay the bills.

I was going through this scenario with a friend and he looked at me and said "My girlfriend and I have been living in sin."

At first, I thought it was a little strange that he was going to tell me about his sex life but then he continued... "It's what I do every day. Bye honey. Love you. Off to make bricks."

Some thoughts:

If I were to sum up the entire Bible, I might say it's a story of a God who doesn't want people making bricks. And it's not about freeing people so that they can then enslave other people - no it's about no one making bricks under the tyrannical rule of power and certainty and comfort.

All are mean masters. It's about being free.

Jesus shows up on the scene and his followers basically say, "Hey who are we going to force to make bricks for us now?" And

Jesus answers, "No one, you idiots. Are you still not getting this? No one is making bricks!"

I came to set the captives free.

If we can be bold with God about anything - and I do think there are certain instances where we are to ask and know that God will give us - it is about being free. No, it's not about getting a new car or a parking spot. It is about being freed from making bricks.

God doesn't want anyone making bricks. Period. When you pray, if you pray, demand God get you out of brick-making and prevent you from forcing others to make them.

Don't be fooled. There are some very rich people making more bricks than some very poor people. It's got little to do with dollar bills and more to do with addiction to the things that dollar bills provide. That's why we don't like the desert where those things are suddenly taken. And yet, that's where we learn everything.

Heroes go into the desert because they are tired of making bricks.

One last word: the capitalistic beatings of America are tearing up our skin as bad as any of Pharaoh's whips. Don't' be fooled. Many of us are working to build monuments to power, to abuse, and to the elite. Arguably, at least Pharaoh was open about it and not hiding it under the less insulting names of free market individualistic pursuit of happiness.

079

stop again.

Those people who were enslaved by a system of production and making bricks... Day after day? As they continued to make bricks, the quotas became larger. As quotas always do.

As they continued making bricks and not reaching their quotas, they were called lazy. As we always are by a system that demands production.

As soon as they were led into freedom they were given a list of words that were meant, in my opinion, to guide them to the discovery of the true gifts of the world. (Some calls these the 10 commandments - which is a terrible way to talk about these words.)

Regardless, one of those words was, basically, "stop".

Can you imagine how that felt?

Stop making bricks.
Stop listening to people who demand more.
Stop listening to people who call you lazy.

Let your brain stop.

You're okay.

Of the massive list of things that the church is generally concerned with, stopping is rarely one of them. In fact, I'm pretty sure it's not even on the top 100 list.

And yet, if we're talking about sin in terms of what hides the divine nature of ourselves, not stopping is one of the biggest obstacles. At least according to the Bible.

Walter Brueggemann talks about "Sabbath" as an active resistant to the systems of greed.

I don't know about you, but the systems of greed in this world drive me crazy and I don't know what to do about them.

Stop is a good start.

Without stopping,

there is no rhythm... or music... it's all just more noise.

When we stop

we acknowledge the world will go on without us. Just fine. When we stop we realize we're enough.

We don't have to do more.

The Sabbath, which began as a day dedicated to stopping - because how else do we ever remember to - began at sunset. I believe the idea behind it was that you would wake up and see that you've been doing nothing and the world is still going. Everyone doesn't need you all the time.

This past week I canceled three events in a row. It was incredibly difficult. I felt guilty. I felt as though I was letting people down. I felt as though Pharaoh was calling me lazy and that I was not producing my quota of bricks.

And then I felt incredibly refreshed. I could think again. I could hear the whispers of the world and of the divine.

I recently read that 42 percent of Americans feel guilty for relaxing.

There is still a Divine power leading us to a place of freedom and breath and refreshment... of stopping. The force has always been leading captives to freedom.

080

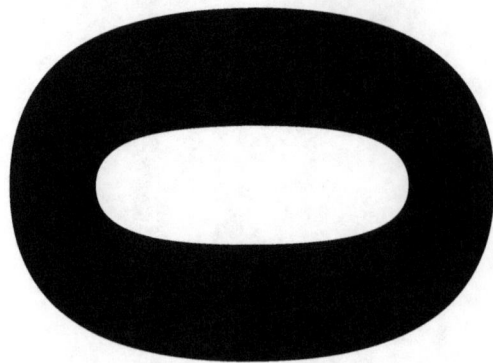

it can be "that good".

Sometimes we get too smart for ourselves.

I've heard people say that since we humans want there to be something for us after we die, somewhere great, it would make sense that we would make that up and thus, it can't be true, because that would just be too much like something we would want to be true.

I don't know if heaven exists or not. I do know that just because I want it to and it seems like a great idea, is a terrible reason to believe it doesn't.

The same could be said for everyone on this planet having a decent life. Well, of course that can't exist - that would be too good. It must be unrealistic.

Just because there are these seemingly unattainable dreams, doesn't mean we're all fooling ourselves. It could mean we're all being drawn to something more good.

081

plastic brains.

The brain is always changing. (Yes, one more thing to add to the list of things that is always changing - and to which religion and faith should proudly add its name.)

The brain is growing, shrinking, and reacting to what you're feeding it. This is one of the reasons that people are a tad worried about technology. It changes our brain and when many individuals' brains change, society's collective brain changes.

That is a bit worrying, if I'm honest.

But, this is not always bad. Before the printing press, people generally had a better ability to memorize. They had to. When humans didn't have to memorize, humans could start putting brain power into other arenas. So less memorization but more technological advances.

I wanted to give my sermons without notes. Not memorize per se, but just get up there and be present. In the same way, a good actor can actually start to act when they don't have to memorize their lines anymore, I think a good speaker can speak when they don't have to look at notes and when those notes have embedded in their consciousness.

It was really hard at first. I gave myself little notes and cues and cheats.

Years later, after giving up notes entirely, it's amazing how easy it now is to memorize messages. And I don't say that proudly, I say it amazed at how well my brain has evolved. My brain has actually changed and is now better at certain tasks.

Pretty remarkable.

Yes, the brain can fade fast.

But, it can also do what you want it to do fast.

There was a pretty large study done on eight Buddhist monks who had spent an average of 34,000 hours in mental training or meditation that found their brains were even more plastic, or more capable of change and resiliency.

Meditation also helps.

082

yep, save the planet.

If the world was an apartment building, I'm afraid there would be some really bad roommates and many of them would be Christians.

Worse, they would say that God made the apartment building for us to do whatever we want with and we're moving out in a few years so who cares...

Worse, they would deny claims of science and responsibility because they are afraid of the cost of a little time, a little effort, a little comfort, and a little - or a lot - of money.

Throw out all the theories and politics. The God I believe in, loves the Earth, dwells in the Earth, cares for the Earth and expects the human beings living on it and because of it, to feel the same way.

The Earth does not belong to any of us. It belongs to all of us. When we don't live to make this home better, we're giving a giant middle finger to the divine power in it.

Yes, I will type that again. If you don't care about making this home better for the humans that live in it, you are giving a giant middle finger to the divine power of it.

083

worlds in worlds.

I assume you've heard of Gerek Meinhardt?

How about Matt Pierce?

Maybe Taylor Cummings?

Interestingly enough, all three of these people were or are ranked number one in the world.

Greek Meinhardt is a two-time Olympian and was the first U.S. foil fencer to earn the Number 1 World Ranking in 2014.

Matt Pierce is the North American Champion and competed in the Catan World Championships for North America in 2014. Yes, the board game Settlers of Catan.

Taylor Cummings won the Tewaaraton Award as the best woman's lacrosse player in the United States. It's the Heisman of Lacrosse. She was also the first sophomore to win the award.

It's amazing the worlds there are in the world.

Running.
Swimming.
Biking.
Chess.
Jazz.
Band.
Choir.

Debate.
Investment.
Drama.
Dancing.

The list goes on and on. There are rankings, there are training, there are camps, there are competitions, there are ways to get higher up the ladder.

I meet the most interesting people who are doing some of the most amazing things who never get recognized for anything outside of their world because they aren't in one of the worlds that matter to the larger world.

It's taught me to approach everyone with humility, curiosity, creativity, and the ability to listen... as I never know who I'm talking to. I may have no idea - and they may have no idea - how great we are.

084

again.

Almost every week, I have these thoughts in some order or another... if you do as well, know you're not alone.

I think I'm going to quit.
Someone else can do this job.
I love this job.
People are crazy.
People are awesome.
Let's move to another country.
I can't believe I get to do this.

This sermon is going to kick ass.
Oh man, what am I going to say?
I have nothing to say.
This is not a sermon.
How am I going to come up with that many things to say?
These are just friends you're talking to. No pressure.
I hope everyone is here for this Sunday because it will be the best ever.

That was the best sermon ever.
That sermon was terrible.
Why did I say that?
I wonder if they heard that?
Did you hear that?
Should I go and change the recording before it posts?
Well next week I can be better.
How can I be better than that?

085

the mystics.

I have a friend who grew up in Fallujah, Iraq. He has lived in the United States for a little more than six months.

The other day I asked him if he knew about Sufism. He said he had heard of it.

"Heard of it?" I responded. "What? That's it? Have you heard of Rumi?" We looked up Rumi and he pronounced his name in Arabic - it sounded cool.

I continued, "Rumi was the man! He was an Islamic scholar and theologian. Sufis are the Islamic mystics. How can you not know about them?"

My friend said, "Why do you know so much about these mystics?"

I told him I was one. He asked if Christians had mystics and I said yes. He said what is a mystic?

This whole problem is not just an Islamic problem.

It's Christian, Jewish and all faiths.

I think part of the reason many struggle with Christianity is because they don't believe in the Christian religion anymore. Many would, and do, believe in Christian mysticism.

This all makes for some conflicts in language and thought.

But, I think I'm in good hands. I don't think Jesus was a fan of religion either. I think he was a mystic. Crazy how different it makes the gospels if you think of Jesus as a mystic. They make so much more sense.

So what are mystics? Well all kinds of things but maybe the best definition I've heard is from a Jewish mystic, Rabbi Kushner: "A mystic is anyone who has the gnawing suspicion that the apparent discord, brokenness, contradictions, and discontinuities that assault us every day might conceal a hidden unity."

They value experience over belief.

Knowledge and experience matters more than logic and belief.

We're all connected matters more than we're all individuals.

Peace matters more than violence.

God is everywhere in every thing. Every is a key word.

If you don't get love of God, than it's not worth going anywhere else. Love. Love. Love.

You can see a sunset, you can understand a sunset, and you can actually be present in a sunset. Yeah that last one.

Mystery matters. Paradox too. Not understanding is understanding. Awareness.

Now. It's all that matters. The past is a memory and the future is imagination. This is where God lives. Right now.

If I imagine a bunch of religious people in a room, they are arguing.

If I imagine a bunch of mystics in a room (no matter what religious language or culture they come from) I imagine them talking about experiences and where they've seen God and where God is in each of them.

Christianity is my language and culture and ritual to get me to what matters: experiencing God.

Others have different language that can help.

Some might say, again, where is Jesus in that? I would answer, again, everywhere. Jesus is the way, the truth, and the life... and Jesus got something beyond religion and encouraged others to do the same.

But, the road is narrow. The mystic road has been narrow for centuries in every faith. Just ask my friend from Iraq. And most Christians. And most Jews. But the narrow road is the best at evolving. Or the evolving road. The seeking, knocking, asking road, unafraid of questions.

Others are now saying mysticism is becoming more accessible than ever before. Diana Butler Bass uses the metaphor of the mystics storming the elevator shaft to Heaven (and tearing it down because that elevator shaft is a primitive view of the universe with God up there and us down here.) And I agree. Good things are happening. A spiritual revolution - or evolution - of sorts.

Some names? I would call all of these people mystics, I don't know if they would call themselves that. But read books and listen to these people.

Anthony DeMello
Thomas Merton
Richard Rohr
Peter Rollins
Gregory Boyle
Alan Watts
Elizabeth Gilbert

Rob Bell
Pierre Teilhard deChardin
Cynthia Bourgeault
Paul Coutinho
Jean-Pierre de Caussade
Pema Chodron
Russel Brand
Brené Brown

980

I know nothing and that is exciting!

I just wrote thousands of words about where I'm at. My thoughts and opinions and lessons. One one hand this seems pretty arrogant: here are my thoughts everyone.

Listen to me.

On the other hand, I realize I really know nothing.

There is so much new out there.

New science, new theories, new ideas, new perspectives, new interpretations, new species, new universes, new books, new people, and new experiences.

I have an adrenaline rush thinking about them.

I'm not afraid of not knowing. I hope you aren't either. If you are, ask yourself why. Is the thing you're holding on to that fragile? Do you have to hold on to it that tightly because it's so threatened by everything out there?

If so, how is that anything close to the creative power of the universe?

Too many people have honestly decided that they know all there is to learn. They wouldn't say it but they act it. If you bring a new way to look at the Bible and/or Hell and/or atonement and/or Jesus and/or the divine... and/or climate change, and/or atheism, and/or gun control... they know it all.

I don't.

I'm grateful for what I've learned, grateful that it will probably change, and excited for the journey in discovering more of this amazing thing called life.

I hope you are too because we all need to keep learning, talking, evolving, admitting, and adapting in order to keep swimming, including you.

So, keep swimming... into the more and the new!

087

and then...

A month ago I got two tattoos: one on each arm.

The first is a symbol on my left arm (I'm left handed) that is meant to represent "create". The second is a symbol on my right arm that is meant to represent "evolve". Both symbols contain the equal sign in them, to remind me that we're all equally loved, worthy, of value, created, and capable of evolving to that realization.

It's been about a year between the time I published these blog posts and then re-read them for the layout of this book. As I said in the first part of this book, I wrote this book for me. And re-reading it, I'm glad I did. I was reminded of some powerful perspectives and lessons that I've learned. I was encouraged. Challenged. Persuaded, by myself. Which is a surreal thing.

I've, of course, changed on some things too. But, that's for another time. There's something powerful to putting your ideas and thoughts out there for the world to see, owning them, and knowing they will change at the same time.

All that to say, create and evolve. They are the themes of this book and the themes of my life. I want to keep creating, keep evolving, and keep moving toward recognizing the divine light in us all equally.

This is a part of that journey. Thanks for reading and being on it with me!

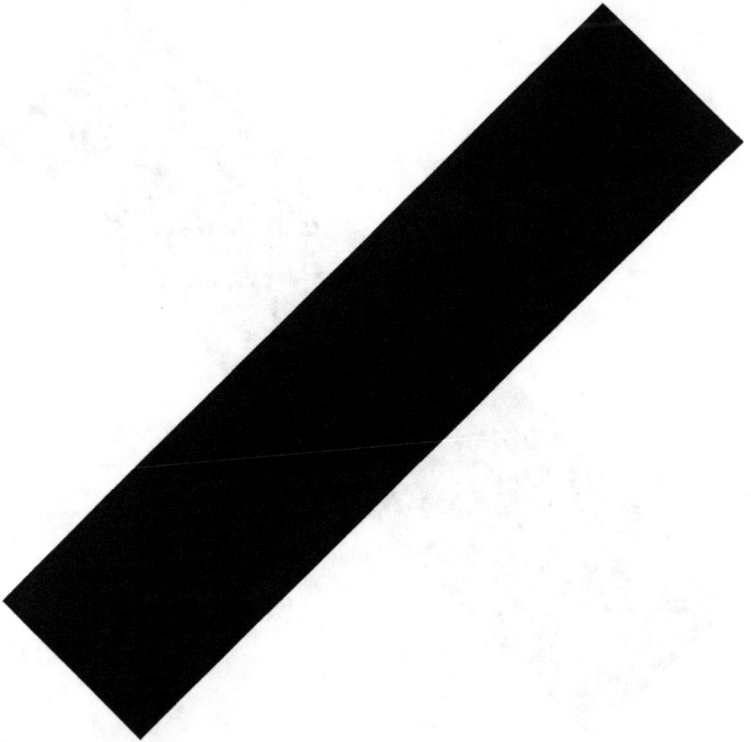

Ryan made video games for 12 years, working for the company Cyan. After that he became a pastor. Video games and pastoring have very little to do with each other except they both involve writing and creativity, two things Ryan likes very much. Ryan is also a graphic designer and helps to run two companies that he and his wife started. Ryan is married to an amazing woman and they have three children. Ryan lives in Spokane, Washington.

Links to the things that Ryan is a part of or has been a part of, as well as the blog where this book originally appeared can be found at:

rsjmiller.com

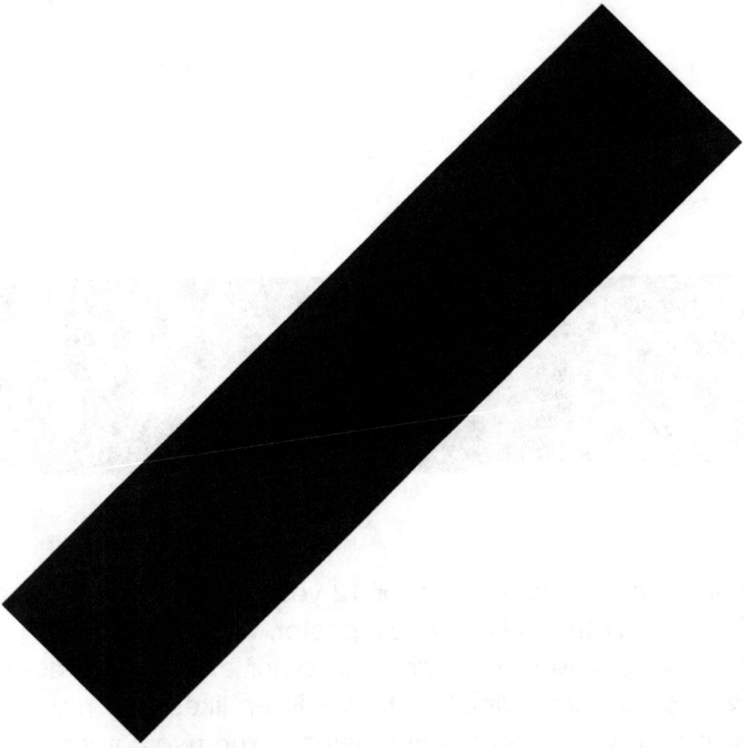

[redacted]

www.ingramcontent.com/pod-product-compliance
Lightning Source LLC
LaVergne TN
LVHW051357080426
835508LV00022B/2867
* 9 7 8 0 9 8 9 5 4 5 4 2 6 *